CONQUER
SPIRITUAL
SPOUSES

J. E CHARLES

Conquer Spiritual Spouses
© 2020 J. E Charles

A publication of Dunamis Christian Center | Upper Room Fire Prayer Ministry

P.O Box 12352 Pleasanton CA 94588

Printed in the United States of America

All rights reserved. No part of this publication may be reproduced, stored in a retrieval system or be transmitted in any form or by any means, mechanical, electronic, photocopying or otherwise without prior written consent of the publisher.

Unless otherwise noted, all Scripture quotations are taken from the New King James Version, copyright © 1979, 1980, 1982 by Thomas Nelson, Inc.

Products are available at special quantity discounts for bulk purchase for sales promotion, premiums, fund-raising, and educational needs.

For details contact us at P. O. Box 12352, Pleasanton, CA 94588 or www.dunamisbookstore.com. Email: sales@upperroomfireprayer.org or Call 408 508 4304

Library of Congress Cataloging in-Publication Data: An application to register this book for cataloging has been submitted to the Library of Congress.

International Standard Book Number:
ISBN: 978-1-7362288-5-2

J. E Charles
Dunamis Publishing House
P.O. Box 12352, Pleasanton, CA 94588 Email: info@upperroomfireprayer.org
Web: upperroomfireprayer.org
Phone: +1 408.508.4304

DISCLAIMER

The information provided in this book is not to be taken for medical or professional advice under any circumstances. By using the information contained in this book, the user assumes full responsibility for his or her actions and agrees that Pastor J. E. Charles will not be held liable or responsible for any consequences that come as a result of the actions taken based on reading the information contained herein.

The reader understands that no promises of success are made to the readers of this book. By reading this book you agree and understand that nothing said herein is meant to give medical, legal, or financial advice and should not be used in place of medical, legal, or financial advice from a qualified expert. If you are in need of legal, financial, or medical help, seek professional help and do not use the information in this book as a substitute for the guidance and advice of certified, qualified experts under any circumstances. Always be sure that you adhere to and obey the government, the laws, and the authorities of your country.

DEDICATION

To the person of the Holy Spirit,
Who is the very reason for my being
And
To my children, living Faith and Ike, who should carry
this message of the gospel of Christ to their generation.

ACKNOWLEDGMENTS

Hereby acknowledge the contributions of all men of God whom God has used in the past and who are still being used by God to prepare me for the coming of our Lord Jesus Christ.

Furthermore, I hereby acknowledge Dr. D.K. Olukoya, an apostle and prophet of God, who understands the power of persistent prayer, whose ministry has seriously blessed my family and revolutionized the act of prayer in our generation. May the Lord keep them 'til the day of His coming.

I salute my wonderful wife, Lady Akuss, for her invaluable support in the ministry. I appreciate her unquantifiable love and support.

CONTENTS

Introduction xi
How to use this book xv

PART 1
UNDERSTANDING THE MYSTERY OF SPIRITUAL SPOUSES

Chapter 1	Who is a spiritual spouse?	1
Chapter 2	Kinds of spiritual spouses	11
Chapter 3	Exposing the agenda of spiritual spouses	15
Chapter 4	How evil covenants are formed	21
Chapter 5	Spiritual marriages	 27

PART 2
ENGAGING IN SPIRITUAL WARFARE AGAINST SPIRITUAL SPOUSES

Chapter 6	Revoking evil marriage sex exchange	37
Chapter 7	Severing covenant with spiritual spouses	 45
Chapter 8	Dealing with tormenting spirits	 57

Chapter 9	Rejecting demon spouses.................................. 67
Chapter 10	Dealing with the seeds/offspring of demon spouse.. 75
Chapter 11	How to establish covenant with god 87
Chapter 12	Finding and choosing a godly spouse........... 97
Chapter 13	Deliverance prayers against evil marital attractions or strange women/men... 107

21 days Prayers to Conquer the Spiritual Spouses............121
Notes 129
Author Information 131
More books from J.E Charles 133

INTRODUCTION

What is life without its attendant challenges? More importantly, what's the essence of living when you can't find a solution to a logic-defying problem? One of life's mysteries that defy logic is spiritual spouses. And the solution to the *silent killer* is in this book: CONQUER SPIRITUAL SPOUSES (Incubi and succubi).

Spiritual spouses are real-life situations. It's not a topic often discussed, which makes it more delicate. When people talk about it, they often describe its horrible effects on how the devil and his cohorts seek to torture their hapless victim. People who embrace the quick but ineffective solution of consulting with a voodoo priest or use magical powers will only cause more havoc. Oh, how painful it is to add salt to a wound! That's what it is like.

In addition, when talking about a solution, our science-driven world doesn't help either. Although science tries to give a reasonable explanation for things that happen in the physical world and proffer probable solutions to problems, it can neither discard the operation of spiritual spouses nor find a way out. At best, science can only discredit the evidence attesting to spiritual spouses as a societal problem; it cannot prove it does not exist. So, most times, victims are left at the mercy of their captors.

Truly, life is lived on the battlefront by everyone; male and female, single, married, widowed or divorced. As humans, created in God's image and likeness, you're already a target for demonic snipers. And if you're weak and unprotected, you can easily become prey to the hand of destiny-destroying demons.

No wonder there are hidden tears on faces, sighs from deep within, heartaches and regrets from painful memories, and fettering wounds sustained from fighting a defeated battle. Why?

The unfortunate victims of spiritual spouses are either ashamed to speak out and get help from the right source or cannot find the right words to describe the terror they face at the hands of demonic forces. So, they sob in solitude, soliloquize in secret, and resign to fate.

However, I'm glad you've laid your hand on this weapon against the destructive acts of the devil and his agent. Do not despair; there is deliverance upon mount Zion, and God has made provisions for total restoration and recovery.

The solution to spiritual problems is found in spiritual books. And the most important of them all is the Bible. Scriptures say that *"Therefore my people are gone into captivity because they have no knowledge: and their honorable men are famished, and their multitude dried up with thirst" (Isaiah 5:13).*

So, it's time to acquire knowledge from this priceless book. You are reading it because you desire to break free from the captivity of the enemy, or perhaps you know someone who needs to be set free from demonic siege and oppression. Conquer Spiritual Spouses will help you effectively war for new spheres of power so that God's kingdom is established in your life and territorial domain.

Yes! No longer ask questions such as, *Can I get rid of this malady of marriage to spirits,* but instead think about how you can effectively engage the compendium of truth and warfare prayers to silence your enemy. So, gather yourself together and muster your last ounce of energy to fight the battle ahead and win convincingly, once and for all.

Victory started the moment you decided to pick this book to read. Your deliverance is here! Dive in 100 percent. Don't toe-poke and think, *"Oh, I've heard some folks say I can be rescued, but it's mere tautology of words which brings no result."* It's not just meant for a pretty reading experience or coffee-table curiosity, but it's a matter of addressing real-life situations.

This book has been prepared with you in mind. Within its pages, you'll be open to the enemy's tricks and activities and how to sever them. The various chapters will take you through a step-by-step study of what spiritual spouses are: types, agenda, and mode of operation.

Likewise, you will learn how people unwittingly enter into a covenant relationship with demons and how to divorce and conquer demonic spouses and their seeds.

More importantly, you will learn how to keep your freedom. As an added bonus, you will be acquainted with truths on how to find a godly spouse.

So, with principles from scripture and gleanings from real-life cases, you'll be engaged with thought-provoking questions and fiery prayers to help obtain your freedom and deliverance from every tormenting spirit.

God is ready to completely estrange you from all demonic activities in your life. As you read this book, pray along in the spirit. It will keep you fired up.

You've been in the heat of demonic oppression for too long. Now, it's time to break the yoke and start living a happy and meaningful life with sweet memories. It is possible only if you begin now.

HOW TO USE THIS BOOK

Words are only as effective as the open mind of the reader. Get set to go against the narratives of the society. So, you have to detach from our contemporary world's explanation about spiritual spouse for you to actualize what has been revealed here.

You don't need anyone to convince you that you need help. But, more importantly, accept that help is sitting gently within your palms and is ready to show you the way out of spiritual forces.

You need to muster courage and dispel every spirit of fear, *"for God has not given you the Spirit of fear, but of power and love and a sound mind"* (2 Timothy 1:7). Ultimately, you need to believe that Jesus Christ has power over all demons, and He has declared it, saying, *"All power is given unto me in heaven and in earth" (Matthew 28:20).* Jesus' statement of authority reveals that demons – including spiritual spouses – are already defeated! And you can walk right into a life of victory.

It doesn't matter how long you've been struggling with spiritual foes. The only time that matters is now. Just a moment of taking the right decision can be the difference between defeat and victory. And I trust you're all in for victory. It's within your reach. Go for it now!

PART 1

UNDERSTANDING THE MYSTERY OF SPIRITUAL SPOUSES

Chapter One

WHO IS A SPIRITUAL SPOUSE?

Science Versus Reality

Two worlds exist: the spiritual and the physical. However, in today's world, the idea of metaphysical occurrences takes the backseat. Our society is mostly driven by a belief in what agrees with reason.

Whatever does not sound logical and cannot be materially or effectively proven even by scientific research. Any mention of spiritual occurrences interfering with the physical realms is scoffed at. Yet, spiritual forces exist and interfere with our physical world. One such interference is the reality of spiritual spouses. Spiritual Spouses are shapeshifters with the ability to transform themselves through an inherently demonic manipulation, sorcery, spells magic or having the divine inherited ability to take the form of a male or female or any creature in the form an incubus or succubus, who descend upon sleeping women and or men in order to engage in sexual activity with them, which may ultimately lead to deterioration of health, mental state and even death.

There have been various scientific explanations to discredit the real-world experience of spiritual spouses. One such assumption asserts that victims may have experienced a waking dream or sleep paralysis.

A waking dream is an involuntary consciousness where you dream while you are awake or subconscious. During sleep paralysis, you cannot engage your muscles and move your body shortly before falling asleep or shortly after waking.

The phenomenon of sleep paralysis is well-established. When a person experiences it, it feels like an unseen force or body pushes him down, or an invisible personality is in his room. This usually elicits a response of panic and fear.

The scientific explanations disproving spiritual spouses believe people mistake waking dreams and sleep paralysis for real encounters with demons. In addition, a real encounter with a spiritual entity is categorized as a mere hallucination. This hallucination is termed a hypnagogic experience where it is common to experience auditory and visual illusions.

However, various scientific research carried out by "Lewis, James R., Oliver, Evelyn Dorothy, Sisung Kelle" in 1996 concludes that the combination of sleep paralysis and hypnagogic hallucination could easily cause someone to believe that a "demon was holding them down". Nocturnal arousal etc. could be explained away by creatures causing otherwise guilt-producing behavior. Add to this the common phenomena of nocturnal arousal and nocturnal emission and all the elements required to believe in an incubus are present.

Do you find yourself going through any of the spiritual events listed below? Then you might need to take the problem of a spiritual spouse seriously:

- Sexual relationships in dreams.
- Missing one's menstrual period in the dreams.
- Getting married and having a family in dreams.
- Pregnancy in dreams.
- Breastfeeding a baby in the dream.
- Shopping with a man/woman in the dream.
- Seeing a man sleeping by one's side in the dream.
- Miscarriages – having physical or spiritual miscarriages after having sex with spirit spouses in the dream.
- Unpardonable sexual error.
- Demonic dream assistance.
- Playing with snakes, swimming in or around water.

In fact, the problems surrounding spiritual spouses go beyond the highlights above. They extend to problems with married couples and singles.

Within marriage, the husband or wife can experience neglect and hatred by an earthly spouse and difficulties in childbearing. Spirit spouses leave a trail of evil deposits that causes disease such as low sperm count, fibroids, and hormonal imbalance.

For singles, they can frequently experience a series of disappointments, rejection, and jilting in relationships with the opposite sex. They also make wrong decisions on who to marry.

Other problems include acidic poverty, where the victims do profitless hard work, persistent rape, and joblessness.

So, this makes it necessary to consult the religious circle for a more comprehensive exposition on the subject of spiritual spouses.

A Drive to Doom – Sexual Drive, the Gateway for Spiritual Spouses

Survival instinct and sexual urge remain the strongest drive in human life. Man is naturally wired to fight for survival. In the same way, man is made a sexual being for a purpose.

God's original design for sexual intercourse is for man to procreate. However, the entrance of sin into the world opened up a rift through which Satan could exploit man's sexual desires and drive him to doom.

There is a spiritual mystery behind sex. As a man and woman engage in sexual intercourse, the physical world meets the spiritual world. This is why it is easy for the devil to enter a man's life through sex.

Sexual intercourse is a covenant between a man and a woman. God's original intention is that sex may bind the husband and wife as one, in body and soul.

By wicked manipulation, the devil has put many people under conscious or unconscious bondage. Several people involve themselves in active and passive participation in spiritual, sexual intercourse because they opened their life to Satan's influence.

A spiritual spouse is a demonic spirit that marries a human spirit, usually through the dream realm, sexual intercourse, or evil yoking. A spiritual spouse usually uses the face of familiar persons to sleep with individuals in their dreams.

It is an abomination for a spirit to marry a human being. God created Adam and Eve and not Adam and a spirit or dog or monkey. By marrying a fellow human being, human beings are deemed to abide by divine statutes.

The Bible says, *"What? Know ye not that he which is joined to a harlot is one body? For two, saith he, shall be one flesh"* (**1Corinthians 6:16**).

In situations when you probably get married or have sex in your dreams, it's a clear indication that an evil spirit is involved. The Bible clearly states that *"while men slept, his enemy came and sowed tares among the wheat, and went his way"* (**Mathew 13:25**).

The first reference to a union between spirits and humankind is found in the book of Genesis.

> *"And it came to pass when men began to multiply on the face of the earth, and daughters were born unto them, that the sons of God saw the daughters of men that they were fair; and they took them wives of all of all which they chose. And the Lord said, My spirit shall not always strive with man, for that he also is flesh: yet his days shall be an*

> *hundred and twenty years. There were giants in the earth in those days; and also after that, when the sons of God came in unto the daughters of men, and they bear children to them, the same became mighty men which were of old. Men of renown. And God saw that the wickedness of man was great in the earth and that every imagination of the thoughts of his heart was only evil continually"*
>
> **(Genesis 6:1-5).**

We know that angels are spirits. So, an intimate relationship between a man or woman and any of these creatures is an abnormality in the design of God for man. This event happened to be the grand opening for subsequent abuse of God's order concerning marriage and a long-time battle between good and evil. And it's why you are reading this book! You're set to mark the line between the good and bad; come on the side of truth and victory!

Two Sides of the Same Coin: Succubus and Incubus

Asmodeus is the spirit responsible for making marriage and sexual intercourse in the spirit realm. It has a female and a male version.

The female version is called Succubus. It is the demon that has sexual intercourse with a sleeping man in his dream. She uses either the face of his wife or someone close to him.

The male version is called Incubus. It is the demon that sleeps with a woman in her dream. This happens because somewhere along the lines, there is an evil marriage that took place. These demons are usually marine-related.

One may have a dream where he sees himself getting married. However, I will not hesitate to say that it is an evil covenant that is being established. That individual wakes up feeling great, unbeknownst to him that he has been unionized to a demon that will derail his destiny and cause setbacks in his life.

Spiritual spouses are evil and do not come from God. They are thieves as they steal what belongs to earthly spouses. Besides that, each time he or she has sex with someone in the dream, there is only one agenda: to kill, steal, and destroy. (John 10: 10)

It is there to pollute an individual's spirit, soul, and body: to kill their physical marital relationships and to steal good things from someone's life, such as virtues. As a result, major breakthroughs are aborted after having sex with them in their dreams. Covenants are also consolidated, and victims are initiated into evil associations in this way. Every time an individual encounters goodness and breakthroughs, they are taken away from him.

It's important to be aware that the spirit husband or wife's activity does not hinge on a victim's promiscuity or urge for sex. Usually, the spirit husband or wife operates in terms of an evil covenant sealed, right under their noses or behind their backs. It could arise as an affliction of the enemy to truncate the victim's destiny.

Attributes of spiritual spouses

- They are extremely stubborn, aggressive, and dangerous.
- They are always persistent and work towards keeping their victims captive.
- They are persuasive when influencing their victims to do ungodly assignments.
- They are persistent in attacking their victims.
- They are liars and masters of deception
- They have two types of gifts (physical and supernatural).
- Mystery of Sex

Categories of Spiritual Spouses

The following are some of the categories of spiritual spouses:

- Conscious ones
- Unconscious ones
- Spiritual prostitutes
- Wandering spirits
- Internal ones

The unconscious ones outnumber the conscious ones. Why is that? It's because they know that if a person ever wakes up or discovers their subtle operations, they will take the nudge to deal with the situation. Hence, they try to keep their impacts secret or make their prey feel like their operation is no big deal.

The Ladders that Invite Spirits Spouses

Spirit spouses can easily be drawn to an individual when he or she engages in some of these;

- Parental initiations
- Sexual perversion
- Fornication
- Masturbation
- Pornography
- Flirting
- Seductions
- Perverse thoughts and evil imagination
- Loose conversations with the opposite sex
- Lust of the eye
- Oral sex
- Anal sex
- Indecent or seductive dressing

How One Acquires a Spiritual Spouse

- ✓ Through seeking satanic protection
- ✓ Through immoral acts
- ✓ Unprofitable gifts
- ✓ Through cultural dances
- ✓ Soul Ties

- ✓ Unholy sexual dresses
- ✓ Through watching pornography and masturbation
- ✓ Through evil dedication

HOW SPIRITUAL SPOUSES OPERATE

Spiritual spouses may take the form of people in the house of God. They pretend while in the church. They do not want to do anything for God as they are dead and are just there as agents of darkness and are planted there to cause havoc. However, God will disappoint them.

Some people have been converted to something in somebody's house, such as flowers. Somebody may take a picture of a Christian and perform some rituals against him, such that they work so hard and gain so little. This is because something somewhere is representing them.

Meditate on this: The case of a spiritual spouse is real. If you have doubted it, it's time to think again.

Do this: Do a thorough check of the occurrences in your life to see if there are any manifestations of the spirit spouse.

Pray this: Lord Jesus, thank You for enlightening me to the reality of spiritual spouses. Shield and deliver me from any affliction by a spiritual spouse.

Chapter Two

KINDS OF SPIRITUAL SPOUSES

There are varieties of spiritual spouses. This chapter highlights them so that the reader can see if they can relate with any of the manifestations.

Physical Spirit Spouse – They tag along with you wherever you may go. They act as monitoring spirits.

Incestuous Spirit Spouse – Incest involves sexual relations between close relatives, especially immediate family members. This is considered a taboo. The case of an incestuous spirit spouse happens when any of the family members is a member of a demonic cult. For instance, witchcraft, occult masonic societies.

Transferred Spirit Spouse - This happens when you share someone else's personal stuff like soap, sponge, clothes, and shoes. Innocently, you can be a partaker of a spiritual spouse through this seemingly innocent act.

Woman Astral Spirit Spouse – This engages every form of demonic and astral powers to achieve its desire. They make use of occultic fuels to get intimate with you. Once they have decided to make you a target, every possible means will be deployed to have sex with you in the dream or otherwise.

Leviathan Spirit Spouse – The most senior in power. It operates through marine activities and is very stubborn to get rid of.

Serpentine Spirit Spouse – It operates through snake spirit and can be very vicious.

Imagination Spirit Spouse – with this spirit spouse, you are left in doubt as to whether the sex took place or it was just your imagination playing tricks on you. You felt something, but you aren't sure if it was real or not. With these kinds of spiritual spouses, one has to be extra cautious to not be caught unawares.

Animal Spirit Spouse – This spirit husband or wife uses an animal to approach you in the dream. This kind is also very difficult to resist. It appears like you are having sex with an animal.

Ancestral Spirit Spouse – You can also think of this as operating in the form of a familiar spirit. It is inherited from your parents or ancestors and passed down through the generations.

Bloodline Spirit Spouse – These spouses appear in the bloodline just to frustrate marriages.

Multiple Spirits Spouses – This occurs when a spirit gains access to you, and then he goes and gathers other demon spirits and brings them to have sex with you. It's like a gang rape situation.

Hidden Spirit Spouse – They do not make love with anyone, but they just go around causing sicknesses and withholding breakthroughs.

Marine spirit Spouse – Marine spirits, also known as Aquarius spirits, mermaid spirits, water demons.

Giant spirit spouse: *as seen in* Genesis 6: 2

Projected spirit spouse: These are witchcraft powers, voodoo powers who project human beings into the dream world through the silver cord by the assistance of a familiar spirit.

Deity spirit spouse: These are strange gods or a deity from evil altars; they visit and torment worshippers with sex.

Dwarf wife or husband: They are little demons that take the image of a child, defiling women and men. They suck the breast of their victims and cause barrenness.

Strongman wife or husband: Strongmen are the generals behind every spirit spouse, and they call themselves owners of mighty and terrible powers.

Old man or woman: Takes the shape of the force of older men and women to torment their victims, and the consequences of the activities is making the victims appear old.

Hidden spirit spouse: They operate behind the scene; they are not interested in sexual gratifications, rather they block an individual's blessings and hinder them from prospering in life. They are very difficult to identify.

Witchcraft or warlock or Warcraft spirit spouse: Anyone who practices witchcraft is associated with demonic spirits, and those consulting them leads to initiation to demonic realms.

Celebrity spirit spouse: People fall in love with media personalities, like top athletes and movie stars.

Manifested spirits spouse: It is an unsuspected case of spirit spouse that manifests in the physical realm.

Graveyard spirit spouse: These are spouses contracted due to the visit to the grave or graveyard or intermittent services.

Forrest or the woods spirits spouse: These are spouses that come from the forest and attract people to themselves.

Other types of spirit spouses include:

Disembodied spirits spouse

Meditate on this: Have you ever experienced any of these manifestations of a spiritual spouse before? Take a trip down memory lane.

Do this: Go over this chapter again and see if there is any you know about or have seen which was not listed.

Pray this: Father, I ask that You separate me from every form of demonic influence and association.

Chapter Three

EXPOSING THE AGENDA OF SPIRITUAL SPOUSES

Nothing happens in life without a purpose. Likewise, spiritual spouses have a purpose and an agenda for their operations in the lives of men. Although many deny the reality of the spiritual world, it is just as real as the natural or physical world.

What happens in the spiritual world affects us today. Every time one has intercourse in his dreams, it is because the demons want to make babies. The *incubus* and *succubus* are not natural but spiritual.

They program *someone* to mess their destiny and everything they have. These set of spirit spouses appear so real that one may believe that they are truly human beings. They come as unconscious spouses, and when they have finished their agenda, they go away. The Bible tells us that the enemy has an agenda.

> *"The thief cometh not, but for to steal, and kill, and destroy: I have come that they might have life and that they might have it more abundantly."*
>
> **John 10:10**

The spiritual spouse is a thief. He holds people captive through vows. That is why everyone needs to make sure that they withdraw any spiritual spouse that they may have made consciously or unconsciously.

Unraveling the motives behind the activities of spiritual spouses

Some of the reasons and agenda behind the activities of spiritual spouses are emphasized below.

1. Initiation:
   By having sex with you, you become one with the spirit.
2. To shake away one's virtue.
3. To sap the power of God operating in the life of an individual.
4. Marital Delay
   They stand at marital gates and bring about a delay or a total hindrance to one's marital bliss. Simply put, they may block a person's chances of ever getting married.

5. To pollute a person's spirit.
6. To make marriages to be barren.
7. To control the life of people negatively.
8. To destroy people's lives through evil dreams.
9. They are very cruel, and they might kill.
10. They make life difficult for people and are very jealous.
11. They block good things in the life of people and family.
12. They bring bad luck and disappointment to people's lives.

Symptoms and Damages Caused by Spiritual Spouses

The presence of a spiritual spouse in life has a lot of negative implications. Some of these are listed below:

- Total obstruction to an individual's life of marital bliss.
- Barrenness in women and low sperm count and impotency in men.
- Because of their jealousy, they'll hinder their victim from getting any suitor—if it's a male spirit. He chooses to exercise complete dominion and ownership over the life of its victim. He makes it abominable for them to be able to find love in the arms of another man.

- Bring about a fatal blow to one's destiny. A spiritual spouse's continuous activities in life will bring about a great catastrophe in such a life.
- The presence of a spirit spouse in a life brings about undue rejection in the life of its victims. You suddenly face rejections anywhere you go for no particular reason.
- Unimaginable and scary nightmares also become a frequent experience. They may begin to dream of serpents, crabs, and scorpions.
- They will cause frustrations in finances and other aspects of an individual's life.
- They cause sicknesses.
- They cause divorce in marriages, as a lot of ladies and gentlemen manage to get married, but afterward, the marriage decays exponentially, like rotten fruit.
- For a spiritual husband, if a man eventually gets to marry his victim, he can render such a man impotent.
- They will put up bouts of fight and warfare through various means, all in a bid to stake their claim on what they think is rightfully theirs.
- They are responsible for the confusion and unnecessary arguments in the home. Suddenly, a home filled with love and serenity becomes a battlefield where strife and wrath are the order of the day. They drown every bowl of love left.
- Seeing yourself pregnant in the dream when you are not married physically. Pregnancy in the dream for a single is a sign that one has a spirit husband.

- Missing one's menstrual cycle in the dream.
- Backing a baby or breastfeeding one in the dream when you don't have yet in the natural.
- Seeing yourself having a family in the dream.
- When you have a dream where you are shopping with a man or a woman.

Meditate on this: Are you experiencing any of the symptoms listed above?

Do this: Try to have a word with your pastor or a spiritual mentor, discussing your recent findings about the spiritual spouse with them.

Pray this: Dear God, I have seen that the enemy desires to steal, kill, and destroy me. I pray that every agenda of the enemy in my life be frustrated in Jesus name. Amen.

Chapter Four

HOW EVIL COVENANTS ARE FORMED

Covenants are a crucial part of our life on earth. A covenant simply refers to a pact or a binding agreement between two or more parties. A woman and a man at the point of marriage make a covenant of life with one another. A father can make a covenant with his son or daughter (Proverbs 4:1-4).

Humans can make a covenant with one another; likewise, a spirit and a man can make a covenant. Based on this principle, we have two categories of covenants. The covenant of God with a man *and* the covenant established by the devil (and his demons) with a man.

God and Man

"And when the fowls came down upon the carcasses, Abram drove them away. And when the sun was

going down, a deep sleep fell upon Abram; and, lo, a horror of great darkness fell upon him. And he said unto Abram, Know of a surety that thy seed shall be stranger in a land that is not theirs, and shall serve them; and they shall afflict them four hundred years; and also that nation, whom they shall serve, will I judge: and afterward shall they come out with great substance. And thou shalt go to thy fathers in peace; thou shalt be buried in good old age. But in the fourth generation, they shall come hither again: for the iniquity of the Amorites is not yet full. And it came to pass, that, when the sun went down, and it was dark, behold a smoking furnace, and a burning lamp that passed between those pieces. On the same day, the LORD made a covenant with Abram, saying, unto thy seed has given this land from the river of Egypt unto the great river, the river Euphrates."

Genesis 15:11-18

A little background information into what transpired in the verses above. In the preceding verses, Abraham had called on the Lord and asked Him about the way out of his present predicament- childlessness. Earlier on, God promised to give Abraham a child—a son from his bowels by his wife, Sarah.

At this juncture, Abraham was definitely at the point of exhaustion. And so, God made a covenant with him to encourage and assure Him. With this, Abraham received an anchor on which he could hang his faith.

In a similar vein, the devil also makes a covenant with men and vice versa. Most times, this is often done out of the victim's scope of awareness or consent. This type of covenant is referred to as an evil covenant. It's an agreement between two or more parties bound by evil powers and a monitoring spirit. On the flip side, it can be an agreement between a man and Satan.

Devil and Man

> *"Because ye have said, **we have made a covenant with death**, and with hell are we at agreement; when the overflowing scourge shall pass through, it shall not come unto us: for we have made lies our refuge, and under falsehood have we hid ourselves."*
> **Isaiah 28:15**

Evil covenants have certain categories:

- Conscious evil covenant
- Inherited evil covenant
- Evil foundational covenant
- Forced covenant through a dream
- Cataleptic evil covenant (this can be initiated by witchcraft powers).

There are various ways that an evil covenant is established. Some of these are explained below.

- Appending your signature on documents in the dream

  You may find yourself signing documents in the dream. Maybe for a job or for whatever it is you have been longing for.

- Engaging in sex in the dream

  This is one of the widely employed ways the devil puts people in bondage of an evil covenant. Many times, people might find themselves having sex in the dream. This is a deep spiritual practice through which many covenants have been established. It could be sex with a familiar spirit disguised as the legal earthly spouse or another evil spirit.

- Holding hands, kissing, shaking hands, and hugging strangers in your dream.

  You may also see yourself walking with or getting married to a familiar spirit in your dream.

- Receiving instructions from a dead loved one or just dreaming about them.

  This is a very common experience people often share with me. Often, people narrate their ordeal to me of how they've seen a loved one who is deceased, give them a message, asking them to sign something, or attempting to take them somewhere.

- Receiving jewelry

  Receiving jewelry such as bracelets, crowns, chains, or rings in your dream are ways in which you might get attached to an evil covenant.

- Through blood
  Blood has always been a very powerful medium through which covenants are made. This could be through animal sacrifice, drinking blood, sex, etc.
- Eating in the dream
  Eating in the dream is another graphic example of how an evil covenant gets established.
- Carrying evil sacrifices
  When one carries an evil sacrifice, maybe a ritual, he/she is invoking an evil spirit, and these spirits would gladly come close to enact a covenant by virtue of the offering made.

Meditate on this: Making covenants in the dream is weird, but it happens! Have you had any such experiences?

Do this: As much as you can remember, check if there was ever a time when you had a strange dream with a significant effect on your life.

Pray this: I break every marital covenant with the spirit spouse, in the name of Jesus!

CHAPTER FIVE

SPIRITUAL MARRIAGES

"And the two will become one…"
Mark 10:8

Earthly marriages join two flesh together to become one flesh. But spiritual weddings drill deeper than that; participants become joined to become one spirit! People who interface with spiritual spouses become one with the specific spirit.

It's interesting to know that marriage is not human-made or demon-made, but God-made. God created the institution of marriage to perform a divine purpose. But many have highly abused this platform. Marriage represents the unity on the physical, mental, and spiritual planes that exists between a man and his wife.

The coming together of two different individuals demands that there should be a level of cohesion. This kind of cohesion is what we see in the Trinity- God the Father, the Son, and the Holy Spirit. There is a perfect blend of the three natures in one. And marriage was supposed to model this pattern.

Unless there is a decision to make a union spiritual—build it up on Godly and Biblical principles—such a relationship may end up as a heartache instead of being a joy and a soothing balm.

Evil spiritual marriage occurs when you marry your soul to a demonic spirit. This is normally done in the dream realms through sexual intercourse or evil yoking. And this leads to demonic love. The scripture clearly warns;

> *"Be ye not unequally yoked together with unbelievers: for what fellowship hath righteousness with unrighteousness? And what communion hath light with darkness? And what concord hath Christ with Belial? Or what part hath he that believeth with an infidel? And what agreement hath the temple of God with idols for ye are the temple of the living God; as God hath said, I will dwell in them, and walk-in them, and I will be their God, and they shall be my people. Wherefore come out from among them, and be ye separate, saith the Lord, touch not the unclean thing: and I will receive you. And will be father unto you, and ye shall be my sons and daughters, saith the Lord Almighty."*
> **2 Corinthians 6:14-18**

When there is a marriage with a demon, the soul is joined to the spirit. The demon goes on to marry one's spirit, and when God sees that, He releases the mind to the devil. Such a mind becomes desperately perverse, wicked, and unrighteous. Take time to pray that you may be delivered in the mighty name of Jesus Christ.

EVIL SPIRITUAL MARRIAGE

The first case of an evil spiritual union is recorded in the Bible. The story goes like this:

> *"And it came to pass when men began to multiply on the face of the earth, and daughters were born unto them, that the sons of God saw the daughters of men that they were fair; and they took them wives of all which they chose. And the Lord said, My spirit shall not always strive with man, for that he also is flesh: yet his days shall be a hundred and twenty years. There were giants in the earth in those days; and also after that when the sons of God came in unto the daughters of men, and they bear children to them, the same became mighty men which were of old, men of renown."*
> **Genesis 6:1-4**

The sons of God here refer to angels who brought forth children with a human. This means that a spirit can sleep with a woman and have a child.

A case study

There is a case in Africa of a creature that came from the waters and married a man. The creatures would come out of the water and dance, shaking their bodies at about 4 a.m.

A man saw these creatures that looked like beautiful ladies dancing in the morning at the beach and hid by the bush to watch them. He said, "Wow!" Then one day, he summoned courage such that he ran and grabbed one of the ladies. When the time came for her to go back to the water, she couldn't.

Then the man and woman made an oath (it is, therefore, possible for a man and a deity to make an oath- a covenant). The deity and the man had four to five children. Regrettably, one day as they strolled in after a walk, something strange happened. When the woman went in to take a shower, she turned into a mermaid. Before the man realized it, the woman disappeared, taking with her all the children.

Deities can have relationships and children with men. Many are married to deities who appear to have a human body.

> *"And God saw that the wickedness of man was great in the earth and that every imagination of the thoughts of his heart was only evil continually. And it repented the LORD that he had made man on earth, and it grieved him at his heart."*
> **Genesis 6:5-6**

God was angry because of the offspring birthed for the giants or Angels. These are known as the fallen angels. They fell off from heaven and dropped in different places on the earth. Those who sunk in the waters were referred to as water demons, while those who landed on the rock are rock demons. They took refuge everywhere they fell. No wonder! They are mostly referred to as fallen angels.

Most people, especially women, have seen their spirit husband come to them physically, and these instances are deep. In occultic cases, some demons physically engage in sexual intercourse with women. There are instances where people are introduced to demons and are forced to marry these spirits. And sometimes, a covenant is made during the wedding, and a ring and other paraphernalia are introduced. All these strange cases lead to spirit husband and wife habitation for them and their children.

At other times, familiar spirits have sex with females and impregnate them. So, new familiar spirits are formed from the womb. This normally happens when parents of the victims have been involved at one point or the other in their lives in carrying sacrifices, rituals, consulting herbalists and mediums, had incisions, or been attacked with witchcraft.

Right from there, the familiar spirit gets into the person's life as a spirit spouse and deal with their victims when it's time for them to bear children. These spirits excessively molest their victims sexually in their dreams. To the extent, when one gets born again, the spirit spouse hides in there until they are dealt with.

Beyond the knowledge of many, there are countless familiar and occultic spirits in the world today that put on the form of men and women to attract them and sleep with them. Often, these people appear familiar and are so eye-catching. They are seductive so much that men and women easily fall prey to them. When one has sex with them, they are automatically married in the spirit, and the life of that person will be greatly afflicted.

Even if the person leaves the partner, the spiritual, marital tie will still be in place. That is why God cautioned against sex before marriage (fornication) and sex outside marriage (adultery) because when one falls into these spirits through sex, it might be difficult to turn back.

But if a wedding or marriage occurs before sex, the spirit would not be able to attract the other person's life as they are legally married and became one. Godly marriage happens when both families sit while vows are exchanged, after which you're welcome you into their families.

SIGNS OF SPIRITUAL MARRIAGES

There are various signs that serve as a pointer to know if an individual is a victim of spiritual marriage. These include;

- Lust
- Heavy seduction
- Masturbation
- Inability to have children
- Sex in the dream
- Hatred

- Rage or temper
- Sexual perversion
- Slavery
- Rejection
- Bestiality or desire to have sex with animals
- Occult activities
- Stagnancy and inability to breakthrough
- Weakness and Tiredness
- Sexual harassment (spiritual and physical)
- Heaviness

Meditate on this: Could it be that at one point or the other in your life, you got caught up in an evil union?

Do this: Check all your relationships to date and look out for the signs of an evil union. Check if there are any of the signs of an evil marriage manifesting in your life.

Pray this: I break free from any evil spiritual marriage; I'm entangled with in Jesus's name.

PART 2

ENGAGING IN SPIRITUAL WARFARE AGAINST SPIRITUAL SPOUSES

Chapter Six

REVOKING EVIL MARRIAGE SEX EXCHANGE

There is a high tendency for strange impacts to imprint on a spiritual spouse victim's life. This is due to an intimate connection with strange, demonic spirits that culminates in several *exchanges* such an individual's life. This exchange takes place through various channels, and it will not leave the victim the same.

The scripture already established that when a man and woman come together as husband and wife, there's a great spiritual mystery playing as they become one flesh. This is also what happens when a man is in union with a spirit- they become one!

> *"And they twain shall be one flesh: so then they are no more twain, but one flesh."*
>
> **Mark 10:8**

EVIL EXCHANGE VIA MARRIAGE

To *exchange* means to take out something completely and replace it with another. This is a strategy that the enemy has continued to use successfully. There is an evil exchange or satanic transfer.

It is possible for virtues to be stolen or replaced, and marriage is a vehicle of exchange. So, when there's a union between two individuals (e.g., man and a demonic spirit), there is bound to be a case of an evil exchange.

VIRTUE TRANSFERRED AND EXCHANGED

Various places in scripture give examples of cases where spiritual inheritance and virtues are passed across between two individuals. A father can pass on a spiritual inheritance to his children. An example of this is when Jacob blessed the two sons of Joseph- Ephraim and Manasseh. Jacob was also blessed by his father Isaac in the same way.

> *"And Israel stretched out his right hand and laid it upon Ephraim's head, who was the younger, and his left hand upon Manasseh's head, guiding his hands wittingly; for Manasseh was the firstborn. And he blessed Joseph, and said, God before whom*

my father Abraham and Isaac did walk, the God which fed me all my life long unto his day, the angel which redeemed me from all evil the lads; and let my name be named on them, and the name of my father Abraham and let them grow into a multitude in the midst of the earth. And when Joseph saw that his father laid his right hand upon the head of Ephraim, it displeased him: and he held up his father's hand, to remove it from Ephraim's head unto Manasseh's head. And Joseph said unto his father, Not so, my father: For this is the firstborn; put thy right hand upon his head. And his father refused, and said, I know it, my son, I know it: he also shall become a people, and he also shall be great: but truly his younger brother shall be greater than he, and his seed shall become a multitude of nations. And he blessed them that day, saying, in thee shall Israel bless, saying, God make thee as Ephraim and as Manasseh: and he set Ephraim before Manasseh."

Genesis 48:14-20

EVIL TRANSFERRED AND EXCHANGED
(2 Kings 5:27, Eccl 8:14, Daniel 4:16, Luke 10:5-6)

Just as blessing and virtue can be transferred, evil can also be transferred and exchanged. Consider this:

> *"The leprosy, therefore of Naaman shall cleave unto thee, and thy seed forever. And he went out from his presence a leper as snow."*
>
> **2 Kings 5:27**

In the above scripture, Naaman's leprosy was transferred to Gehazi. This was possible because Gehazi enacted a spiritual covenant when he received gifts from Naaman. This was a form of union. On the wings of the exchange, he became a partaker of Naaman's leprosy, as Elisha pronounced.

EVIL EXCHANGE VIA EVIL MARRIAGE

In marriage as a spiritual union, there is a high level of spiritual exchange that occurs between the parties involved. Some of the exchange includes:

Spirit Exchange

A terrible spirit may enter into a person and take over his personality. There will be constant misfortune. It is possible for someone to be alive while the real essence of the person is gone. The human essence has been withdrawn. Of course, blessings will not come the way of such a person.

Body Exchange

Some people look older than their age. Once some people enter into a place, their presence invites irritation. That is why we often hear testimonies concerning the fact that a whole personality went out of somebody's body during prayer.

Brain exchange

The enemy knows that without your brain, you cannot succeed in your academics. There are many cases in which witches were compelled to remove the intelligence of brilliant people and replace it with the brain of a goat or cow.

Child Exchange

A pregnant woman could be attacked, with her unborn child taken out and replaced with an evil fetus through satanic surgery.

Wealth exchange

This occurs when the money a person ought to make is transferred and exchanged with counterfeit money. The hairs of the individuals are often taken away to manipulate their wealth.

SYMPTOMS OF SATANIC EXCHANGE

- Firstborn demotion.
- Serious failure at the edge of serious breakthroughs.
- Unexplainable health failure.
- Brain failure.
- Memory loss.

- Having children who become your enemy.
- If you are a girlish boyish girl.
- Wrong marriage.
- Stagnancy.
- Dis-favor.
- Vagabond Life.
- Insanity and sad countenance.
- Contrast personality.
- Making unexplainable and unpardonable errors.
- Blackout.
- Horrible nightmares.
- Horrible dreams hinder or prevent good things.
- Desiring good things but unable to carry it out.
- Getting married in the dream.
- Cycle of poverty.
- Having constant failure and disappointment.
- Life of trouble and hardship.
- Seeing dead or mad people in the dream.

Pray these prayers if you notice any of these symptoms in your life.

1. Every spirit husband or spirit wife, I renounce you in the name of Jesus!
2. Every blood and soul-tie covenants enacted with the spirit husband or wife, I break away from you completely in the name of Jesus!

3. Every form of evil marriage sex exchange that has taken place in my life, I wage war against you by fire in the name of Jesus!
4. Every virtue that has been lost or replaced in my life due to an evil union is restored in Jesus name!
5. Every trademark of evil marriage in my life, be shaken out of my life in Jesus name!
6. I declare loudly that I am forever united to Jesus. I am joined to the Lord.
7. I file a counter-report against every evil marriage in my life in Jesus name.
8. Every satanic exhibition be destroyed in my life in Jesus name!
9. I pull down every evil, wicked law working against my life!
10. I decree I'm no longer bound to any evil covenant.
11. I am set free and delivered in the name of Jesus!
12. I declare every hold of the gates of hell on my life is broken in Jesus' name.
13. I call down the fire of the Almighty to destroy every material used in an evil marriage against me, in Jesus name!
14. I withdraw my blood or any other part of my body laid on the altar of spirit husband or wife.
15. I empty myself of every deposit in my life as a result of the evil sexual relation.
16. I redeem myself from every sex and marriage trap in the name of Jesus.

Meditate on this: Are there spiritual graces and blessings you have lost through an evil marriage?

Do this: Make a list of everything happening in your life right now. Check to see if there is a pattern the events are following.

Pray this: I recover everything that the devil has stolen from me. I take it all back in Jesus name. Amen!

Chapter Seven

SEVERING COVENANT WITH SPIRITUAL SPOUSES

A covenant is an agreement between two or more parties. It is a contract with terms spelled out and sanctions attached to its breach unambiguously stated at the outset. Psalms 89:34 reveals that a covenant cannot be broken or altered.

> *"My covenant will I not break, nor alter the thing that is gone out of my lips."*

Covenants are how God chose to communicate to us, redeem, and guarantee eternal life in Jesus. It's how God first decided to deal with Mankind. In Genesis Chapter 2, God made a covenant with man for him to live in obedience with Him. In Chapter 9, God made a covenant with Noah that there would not be another flood. While in Chapter 12,

He made a covenant with Abraham and his descendants. Because God is a covenant Keeper, the covenant still holds today. Up till now, He still curses those who curse the saint and blesses those who do the same.

God never breaks a covenant. Just as He said it, so will He do it!

EXAMPLES OF (SATANIC) DIABOLICAL COVENANT

- Covenant with idols.
- Covenants with water.
- Covenants with the triangular powers (the sun, moon, and stars).
- Covenant with witchcraft.
- Covenants with occult agents or powers.
- Covenants with the land.
- Covenants made with masquerades.
- Covenant made with a rock spirit.
- Covenant made with spirit husband or wife.
- Covenant made with evil trees.
- Covenant made with evil spirit and powers at cross-roads.

HOW THE COVENANT WITH THE DEMON SPOUSE IS FORMED

The covenant with a demon spouse is established via these means:

> **Through Adultery**
>
> Adultery refers to the act of having sex with a man or a woman who is not your lawfully wedded partner. Doing this establishes a bond (covenant) between the parties involved. The Bible in 1Corinthians 6:16 says: *"what? Know ye that he which is joined to a harlot is one body? For two, saith, he shall be one flesh."* This act of unfaithfulness to one's spouse comes with many deadly repercussions on both partners and in their marriage. Having more than one sexual partner with whom one is involved is a great opening for a demonic covenant.

> **By Blood**
>
> The use of blood is one of the most potent ways of establishing a covenant. This is because life is in the blood. Incisions, cuts in the body, marks on the body are all ways of enacting a covenant. The act of lovers cutting each other, mixing the blood with wine in a container to drink is a terrible covenant. This is a means widely adopted by the occult.

> **Counterfeit Religion**
>
> Satan deals in corrupted and counterfeit covenants. Many of the so-called religious houses

and houses of prayers are nothing but a charade of counterfeiters. These are offshoots of demonic agenda, which strives to hold people in bondage as they ignorantly approach them for consultation and solutions. Many unsuspecting individuals have been initiated into a dark, demonic covenant through these routes.

➢ **By Occultic Covenant**

The occult knows about the importance of a covenant. As a result, every member of a cult group is made to swear an oath of secrecy and to pledge their allegiance to the god they serve.

➢ **Through Food and drinks**

Many foods have been offered to demons or a strange god. Partaking of such foods and drinks invariably makes one a party to an existing line of demonic covenant. This is why you need to be careful of what you eat, where you eat, and from whom you eat. A lot of innocent children have been initiated into the occult through food.

➢ **Fashion**

In our world today, the devil is the god of fashion. And he has his devotees meticulously carrying out their duties in this field. Many have been tricked into loose and ungodly modes of dressing. These kinds of dressings do more to attract demon spirits to such individuals.

SIGNS OF SATANIC OR DIABOLICAL COVENANT

1. Repeated evil dreams.
2. Seeing yourself in the midst of familiar or strange individuals and eating with them.
3. Continuous sex in the dream.
4. Appearing in old places such as your old school, your old house, and so on.
5. Encountering deceased loved ones.
6. Constantly failing at the edge of a breakthrough.
7. Having a repeat of cases of stillbirths.
8. Having a crazily abnormal sexual urge.
9. A patterned evil occurrence in your family.
10. Retrogression.
11. Laboring with little or no reward.
12. Engaging in illicit and ungodly acts and finding it difficult to get rid of them like smoking, drinking, telling lies, and a whole slew of others.

STEPS TO BREAKING THE COVENANT OF DEMON SPOUSE

- Give your life to Christ.
- Repent from unknown sins.
- Confess your sins as much as you can remember.
- Break all the covenants you might have made knowingly or unknowingly.

- Flee from sin and other properties that may aid these demons to gain entry into your life.
- Declare your freedom from all satanic oppression.
- Take authority in the name of Jesus and get rid of indecent dressing.
- Separate yourself from unbelievers (ungodly friends).
- Do not commit any form of adultery.
- Do not practice the sin of polygamy.
- Pray recovery prayers.
- Live your new life as a new creature who has been delivered from every satanic covenant.

Basics of Deliverance

Deliverance is like peeling off the skin of the layers of an onion skin. You don't peel all the layers at once during a spiritual deliverance. You peel it one after the other as the Holy Spirit brings it to the surface until all the poison is gone.

As you pass through the journey of deliverance, do not get discouraged in the process. Well. That's what it is—a process! Keep taking those layers off as the Holy Spirit leads until you are clean and whole, as a pure and spotless bride!

The Bible encourages that we should follow God patiently and hold on tightly to His promises. We know He'll fight our battles and win the victory on our behalf.

> *"That ye be not slothful, but followers of them who through faith and patience inherit the promises."*
> **Hebrews 6:12**

> *"But thanks be to God, Which giveth us the victory through our Lord Jesus Christ."*
> **1Corinthians 15:57**

> *Therefore seeing we have this ministry, as we have received mercy, we faint not; but have renounced the hidden things of dishonesty, not walking in craftiness, nor handling the word of God deceitfully; but by manifestation of the truth commending ourselves to every man's conscience in the sight of God. But if our gospel be hid, it is hid to them that are lost: In whom the god of this world hath blinded the minds of them which believe not, lest the light of the glorious gospel of Christ, who is the image of God, should shine unto them.*
> **2Corinthians 4:1-4**

GOD'S WORK OF SEVERING

The good news is: every tree that the heavenly father did not put in our bodies shall be rooted out! The tree may represent things such as poverty, untimely death, infertility, sickness, backwardness, or sorrow, among others. And in this case, a spiritual spouse.

> *"But he answered and said, every plant, which my heavenly Father hath not planted, shall be rooted up."*
> **Mathew 15:13**

A spiritual spouse is a stranger in your life! The more you give them a right of way in your life, the deeper they go in ruining your life.

You should pray that the Holy Spirit may reveal what the evil spirits may have modified to represent themselves in your life. These spirits will reap what they have sowed as they steal from innocent souls.

Make this your prayer

The prayer is:

1. That every tree that God did not plant inside of you should be rooted out!
2. Any evil material that might be planted in your life should die in the name of Jesus!

God's Holy Spirit can ruin every evil plot that the enemy set up. The Holy Spirit's fire can locate and destroy altars built by people with evil intentions so that those afflicted can withdraw their souls from the evil alters.

3. Every string and tie that connects you to spiritual spouses, such as the power of dreams, should break loose by the fire of the Holy Spirit.
4. That God should remove anything planted in your life, such as a wedding ring and wedding certificates, may link you to spirit spouses.

5. Let the fire of the Holy Spirit burn through your body to repair any damages done by the ministry of spirit spouses.

Use the Word!

The scripture is your weapon! Below are some promises of scripture to help you in your conquest. From these passages, you will see your oneness with Christ. As a result of this, no other spiritual entity ought to have a right on your soul.

> *"For thy maker is thine husband; the Lord of hosts is his name, and thy Redeemer the Holy One of Israel; The God of the whole earth shall be called."*
> **Isaiah 54:5**

So, if Christ is your husband, then legally, and according to Him, you cannot have another spirit husband or wife.

> *"But he that is joined unto the Lord is one spirit."*
> **1Corinthians 6:17**

Since you are one with God, you cannot be joined with any other god.

> *"No weapon formed against me shall prosper, and every tongue which rises against you in judgment. You shall condemn. This is the*

> *heritage of the servants of the Lord, and their righteousness is from Me, Says the Lord."*
>
> **Isaiah 54:17**

> *"Behold, they shall surely gather together, but not by me: whosoever shall gather together against thee shall fall for thy sake."*
>
> **Isaiah 4:15**

> *"Ye are of God, little children have overcome the: because greater is he that is in you than he that is in the world."*
>
> **1John 4:4**

Victory is yours in the Lord! All you have to do is to exercise the rights and freedom you have in Christ!

SEVERING TIES WITH THE SPIRIT SPOUSE

Highlighted below are a list of steps you can take to sever all ties completely with a spiritual spouse

- Give your life to Christ.
- Repent from known sins.
- Confess your sins as much as you can remember.
- Break all the covenants you might have made knowingly or unknowingly.
- Flee from sin and other properties that may aid these demons to come through with you.

- Seize authority in Jesus' name and declare your freedom from all satanic oppression now!
- Get rid of every form of indecent dressing.
- Disengage yourself from unbelievers (ungodly friends).
- Runaway from every temptation to adultery or fornication.
- Desist from polygamy.
- Pray some recovery prayers.
- Live the new life as a believer who has the nature of God on the inside.

PRAYERS

Say these prayers to separate yourself from every covenant with spiritual spouse

1. Spirit spouse, discharge me by fire, in the name of Jesus!
2. Every spirit spouse, I dissociate with you, by the blood of Jesus!
3. I break away from every marital covenant with the spirit spouse, in the name of Jesus!
4. I destroy the mirrors, video cameras, and everything that the enemy is using to monitor all of my activities by fire in the name of Jesus!
5. Generational agreements of my lineage troubling my destiny, break by fire in the name of Jesus!

6. Any symbol reinforcing satanic covenant in my life, break by fire in the name of Jesus!
7. I set myself, my glory, my virtues free from the capacity of satanic covenants in the name of Jesus!
8. Any soul tie between me and my father, between me and my mother, break by fire in the name of Jesus!
9. Any authority sponsoring satanic pledges in my family, as I clap my hands, die by fire in the name of Jesus!
10. Every altar receiving animal or human blood to fortify satanic vows against me, I command it to scatter by fire, in the name of Jesus!

Meditate on this: You are God's property. As such, no foreign power has any right over your soul.

Do this: Go through your Bible and write out the scriptures that speak of your oneness with Christ.

Pray this: Dear God, help me to break free from every spiritual stronghold holding me down.

Chapter Eight

DEALING WITH TORMENTING SPIRITS

> *Finally, build up your strength in union with the Lord and by means of his mighty power. Put on all the armor that God gives you so that you will be able to stand up against the Devil's evil tricks.* ***For we are not fighting against human beings but against the wicked spiritual forces in the heavenly world, the rulers, authorities, and cosmic powers of this dark age.***
> **Ephesians 6:10-12(GNB)**

Our warfare is not with humans but with the devil and his agents. They achieve this through heresies, the doctrine of devils (1 Timothy 4:1), hypocrisy, diabolical imagery, amongst others. And the sad part is, some people do not believe that the devil's activities are real.

Thankfully, the Bible reveals that we are constantly in battle with evil spirits. And these spirits are agents of the devil, sent from the pit of hell to wage war against the saints. Ephesians 6:10-12, stated above, reveals that our contender is not visible. And the spiritual realm in which they exist and operation is as real as the physical world. What takes place in the spiritual realm can affect anyone who is not armed with the power of the Almighty God physically. Out rightly speaking, life is more spiritual; it is more that than our physical senses. And we must learn to combat them in the place of prayer.

Because, truthfully, the devil and his cohorts are out to be a pain in the neck of God's children. The scripture says he is "*like a roaring lion, seeking whom he may devour.*" Note that *"whom"* is not a random person, but the believer. He doesn't go after his kind; he's against those who are a threat to his kingdom. Can you guess who it is? You are!

YOUR MIND IS AN ACCESS POINT

You may be wondering how he gets at believers. In reality, the devil is tricky and smart. So, he subtly attacks God's children. He doesn't appear like a monster with two horns and says, *"Hey! My name is Satan, and I'm here to torment you!"* No! He comes like a friend and manipulates his way to your mind. And once your mind has been captured, you've fallen prey. That's the devil target point! He wants to torment your mind and make you question your faith, and ultimately lose conviction in God.

CONQUER SPIRITUAL SPOUSES 59

How does he torment? Through worry, fear, depression, and more. Have you ever heard a voice whispering death to you? Maybe you're ill, and your doctor says there's still hope, yet you keep hearing a whisper, *"you think you'll make it?" "You'll die!"* In a moment, fear grips you, and you begin to worry about things you can't control. Then, within moments, you're gradually drowning in the ocean of depression. This is what the devil delights in doing. On the other hand, even when the doctor says you'll die, it's in your place to cancel it with the word of God!

Perhaps, you could be taking giant strides in your business endeavor, and just when you think that you're on the path to accomplishing the vision you've envisaged. You could find the devil whisper to your mind, *"You'll lose everything!"* no doubt, this will frighten you and may threaten to lose your balance or drift from God. However, be guarded; scriptures remind us that he prowls around seeking for whom to destroy.

Now, it's time to buckle up and bout these spirits of torments! Do you know why you need to take action now? It's because as long as you remain unguarded, you'll give in to their tactics and open up an entry for their activities. The good news is God has given you power and authority over the devil and his agents! And you must constantly exercise your authority and dominance.

YOU'VE GOT THE ARMS!

Over 2000 years ago, Jesus defeated Satan on the cross of Calvary and gave us the power to defeat the enemy! The fact is, Satan trembles at the mention of the name of Jesus because he knows that at the mention of His name, every knee must bow. So, you need to know that the devil and his demons have no right over your life as a believer!

Instead of listening to the devil's taunting voice, fight with the divine weapons you have. However, until you know who you are in Christ, you can't step into the reality of the authority He has given you. And, it will be difficult to exercise and maximize the power He's granted you access to. Remember the instruction, *"Put on the full armor of God!"* Understand that if you're not fully kitted, you're on the losing ends. And, to be completely armed, you must be in Christ!

SPEAK THE WORD!

Bible is the greatest gift that God has given to us. Another powerful weapon is your mouth. These two make a perfect pair for fighting the devil and his cohorts. The Bible is the sword—God's word. It is powerful and true; He can only speak positive things concerning His children. And, your mouth is for claiming, declaring, decreeing, and professing what God says concerning your life.

So, when it seems like you've hit rock bottom and the devil says, *"Give up!"* You begin to claim the promise of God for your life in Isaiah 40: 29-31. You tell him, *"He gives *strength to the weary and increases the power of the weak. Even youths grow tired and weary, and young men stumble and fall, but those who hope in the Lord will renew their strength. They will run and not grow weary; they will walk and not be fault."* By so doing, they pierce that ugly spirit with the sword of truth, and it begins to take off from you.

SATAN DREADS GOD'S WORD

The devil and agents are afraid of believers who are filled with the word of God. So, when they come in contact with anyone armed with the word of God, they know they'll be defeated. But, if you're a Christian who doesn't know the promises of God concerning your challenges, then consider yourself as one who is at the mercy of the devil. God says,

Therefore my people are gone into captivity because they have no knowledge: their honorable men are famished, and their multitude dried up with thirst.
Isaiah 5:13

Sadly, many people have already been held bound by these tormenting spirits and can't find their way to freedom. But the good news is, the scripture provides for a road map that leads to victory. Most importantly, as you tread this path, you must be sensitive to the voice of the spirit for directions. The Bible says that the Holy Spirit is our Guide. So, if you yield to the prompting of the Spirit, you will overcome the wiles of the enemy.

YOU'VE GOT THE SPIRIT

Where the spirit of the Lord is, there is Liberty. If you have the spirit of the Lord in you, He will fill your mind and heart; there will be no room for negative thoughts. You'll just find yourself doing exploits for God and making waves for His Kingdom. And, even when things seem to be rough because you have the Spirit of God in you, there'll be no reason to fear.

> The Bible says, *"Ye are of God, little children, and have overcome them: because greater is he that is in you than he that is in the world.*
> **1John 4:4**

Do you remember when you were younger, how you'd sing, *"When Jesus is in my boat, I'll smile at the storm?"* The same thing applies here! You've got the Holy Spirit! In other words, you've got God! So, you've got all it takes to defeat the enemy! The word GREATER is a comparative adjective which—in this context—is used to liken the magnificence of two unlikely personalities—God and the devil. And, the Bible assures you that you've got God, and He's BIGGER than that tormenting spirit! Isn't that soothing enough?

THEY ARE ALIENS

At every point of confrontation by a tormenting spirit, always remember that Jesus is in you, and His power is at work in you. Nonetheless, you'll have to choose to make His presence and power at work for you. When you acknowledge this reality, you can command evil spirits to leave you in the name of Jesus, and they shall obey you! Jesus says,

> *As soon as they hear of me, they shall obey me: the strangers shall submit themselves unto me. The strangers shall fade away and be afraid out of their close places.*
>
> **Psalms 18:44-45**

Evils spirits are called *strangers*? They are not part of your body. The English Dictionary defines a stranger as "An outsider or a foreigner". This means that tormenting spirits are not resident in your body, so they are outsiders. And, when a stranger visits you at home, it's your choice to either receive or return them. If you don't open the door of your house, they can't have access to your room. Now, you know that the power to either retain or return them is in your hand.

ENGAGE THE PRAISE PHRASE

Another powerful weapon God has given to us is the weapon of praise! Sometimes, praising God in the middle of a crisis is always difficult. How do you praise God when the weight of the world seems to be on your shoulders? Your doctor says you have two weeks to live. You are obese and can't seem to *fit in*. The reality of life keeps tormenting you, and you keep wallowing in the struggles. You're weary because you feel like God feels distant. Painful life blows and losses keep escalating. And the list keeps going!

There is something that can make a lasting difference. And, it's praising Him irrespective of the situation around. Praise causes life-changing miracles and confuses the enemy and his agents. When the evil spirit comes at you, hit back with a praise phrase, *"Thank you, Jesus." "Lord, I adore You." "Glory to your name,"* and more. Understand that when you acknowledge God and worship Him, He steps into your situation and delivers you from every torment.

The praise phrases are like the five magic words—please excuse me, sorry, thank you, and I love you. These words may seem irrelevant because, of course, we can do without them. But, they could attract a good turn, which wouldn't have been possible on a normal day. Praise phrases are short yet powerful!

David reminds us that we should praise God when the road is both smooth and rough. He said,

> *"When I look beside me and see that there is no one to help me, no one to protect me. No one cares for me. I will praise you because of your goodness to me."*
>
> **Psalms 142: 4,7b**

Praise shifts our focus from the problem to the solution—God. By praising God, you prove to Him that He's the only help you have, and you can't dictate for Him what to do. Let me remind you of the story of two people who were captured and tormented, yet they overcame because they praised. They are Paul and Silas.

The Bible reveals that as they sang and prayed in the prison, there was an earthquake that shook the foundations of the prison. It didn't just end there; the prison door opened. What a wonder! What is that thing that is tormenting your life? Is it bonds of uncertainties? Shackles of discouragements? God is telling you to stop striving with your strength and wisdom and just begin to praise your way through to victory?

As you study the word of God, profess it, claim the promises, praise, and pray, may you experience victory on all sides of life. In Jesus' name, Amen!

Meditate on this: We bind principalities and power when we take the word of God in our hands, declare it with our mouths, and proclaim His name with praises. Are you willing to take your hands off of your life, and low God works His miracles through the weapons He's given you?

Do this: Go through the Bible and write out the scriptures that authenticate your victory in Christ. Try to read them out loud to yourself and memorize them. Then, put them in a place where you'll see them often.

Pray this: Thank You, Jesus, for the victory I have in You. I declare that I am no longer a slave to any tormenting spirit.

CHAPTER NINE

REJECTING DEMON SPOUSES

Life is a battlefield, and at the end of every battle, victory is expected. Likewise, in our battle against spiritual spouses, our aim is to anticipate victory and nothing less.

> *Shall the prey be taken from the mighty or the lawful captive delivered? But thus saith the LORD, Even the captives of the mighty shall be taken away, and the prey of the terrible shall be delivered: for I will contend with him that contended with thee, and will save thy children. And I will feed them that oppress thee with their flesh; and they shall be drunken with their blood, as with sweet wine: and all fresh shall know that I the LORD am thy Savior and thy Redeemer, the mighty one of Jacob.*
>
> **Isaiah 49:24-26**

Going through the scriptures, we see various words of admonitions and capsules of strength to help keep the believer full of faith in the face of any adversary. The psalmist, on various occasions, reveals his unwavering faith in the Lord.

> *The LORD is my light and my salvation;*
> *who shall I fear? The LORD is the strength*
> *of my life; of whom shall I be afraid?*
>
> **Psalms 27:1**

The famous chapter of the book of psalms has this to say about the all-time assurance that you can be preserved from the destruction that lay waste by noonday and the terror at night.

> *He that dwelleth in the secret place of the Most*
> *High shall abide under the shadow of the Almighty.*
> *I will say of the LORD; He is my refuge and my*
> *fortress: my God; in him will I trust. Surely he*
> *shall deliver thee from the snare of the fowler, and*
> *from the noisome pestilence. He shall cover thee*
> *with his feathers, and under his wings shalt thou*
> *trust: his truth shall be thy shield and buckler.*
> *Thou shalt not be afraid for the terror by night;*
> *nor for the arrow that flieth by day. Nor for the*
> *Pestilence that walketh in darkness; nor for the*
> *destruction that wasteth at noonday. A thousand*
> *shall fall at thy side, and ten thousand at thy right*
> *hand; but it shall not come nigh thee. Only with*

thine eyes shalt thou behold and see the reward of the wicked. Because thou hast made the LORD, which is my refuge, even the Most High, thy habitation; there shall no evil befall thee, neither shall any plague come nigh thy dwelling. For he shall give his angels charge over thee, to keep thee in all thy ways. They shall bear thee up in their hands, lest thou dash thy foot against a stone...
Psalms 91:1-16

Don't stop to read it here, but finish up the remaining verses; they are divine missiles against the devil. As you do so, your heart will be ignited with fire and renewed passion. And sternly reject every appearance of a demon spouse.

DEMONIC SOUL ROBBERS

Below are a few helpful nuggets about demonic soul robbers.

- In life, there are physical and spiritual markets
- There are markets of darkness where the souls of men are sold.
- There are soul traders, soul hunters, soul advertisers, and soul buyers.
- There are satanic businessmen and women who profit from the sale of souls. For them, it's purely business

- The kingdom of darkness buys and sells the souls of men
- The kingdom of darkness profits from the destruction of men
- Being a product of darkness and not knowing it's disastrous.
- A person can be living while his soul has been sold off
- This strange occurrence is the mystery of evil domination and virtue manipulation

And the merchants of the earth shall weep and mourn over her; for no man buyeth their merchandise any more: the merchandise of gold, and silver, and precious stones, and of pearls, and fine linen, and purple, and silk and scarlet, and all thine wood, and all manner vessels of ivory, and all manner vessels of most precious wood, and brass, and iron, and marble, and cinnamon, and odors and ointments, and frankincense, and wine, and oil, and fine flour, and wheat, and beasts, and sheep, and horses, and chariots, and slaves, and souls of men.

Revelation 18:11-13

Evil Prophetic Manipulation

There are quite a number of ways through which an evil prophetic manipulation comes to play in one's life. Most of these means are subtle and deadly. Let's check out a few of these ways:

- Through fornication or adultery: adultery or fornication is one way through which one can undergo an evil prophetic manipulation. It introduces a great level of disorder to such a life.
- Contamination from the womb: Consumption of demonic food and drinking concoctions can, in the long run, affect a child negatively.
- Idol worship: God's first commandment to the Israelites in Exodus 20:1 is still valid till eternity.
- Anger: This can happen in various ways.
- Household wickedness: There are many examples of this in the Bible. Jesus told us in Mathew 10:36 that the enemies of a man shall be members of his household.

SOME SYMPTOMS OF SOULS IN THE MARKET

- ✓ Blinding headaches
- ✓ Noisy ears
- ✓ Expectations are always cut off
- ✓ A heavy body
- ✓ Loss of important things unexpectedly
- ✓ Feeling battered upon waking
- ✓ Futile prayers

- ✓ Demotion dreams, e.g., dreaming of old schools attended nakedness, etc.
- ✓ Missing correct timing
- ✓ Lack of favor
- ✓ Being singled out for persecution

HOW TO RECOVER A SOUL

- Salvation. You must be genuinely born again
- Repentance- You must be truly sorry for your sins and truly repent from them.
- Warfare -war against the markets and traders to set yourself free.

HOW TO DEAL WITH SPIRITUAL SPOUSES

- ✓ Yield your life to God. He has the power to deal with spiritual spouse. Repent of all sin.
- ✓ Incubate your life with the fire and word of God.
- ✓ Prayer: Pray ballistic prayers like, Oh God, make my life too hot for my enemies to handle.
- ✓ Divorce the spirit spouses by breaking all the covenants keeping the marriage in place using **(Colossians 2:14 and 2 Timothy 4:18)**
- ✓ With the blood of Jesus and the fire of God, detach yourself from the spirit spouse.

CONQUER SPIRITUAL SPOUSES

- ✓ Set all the belongings used to consummate the marriage on fire. For example, the ring, the marriage register, etc.
- ✓ Plead the blood of Jesus to purge any evil deposit in you by the spirit spouse and use the fire of the Holy Ghost to uproot every evil plantation.
- ✓ Return any property of the spirit spouse that could be in your possession to him/her.
- ✓ Retrieve everything that belongs to you that is in the possession of the spirit spouse.
- ✓ Rededicate yourself to God after guaranteeing that all evil dedications have been properly broken.
- ✓ Develop perfect hatred for the spirit spouse and be determined to gain freedom.
- ✓ Consider the content that you watch on your television, reading materials, and manner of dressing.
- ✓ Live a life that pleases God

Pray these prayers as you reject demon spouses

1. Any spirit spouse tormenting me, I declare my release by fire, in the name of Jesus.
2. By the blood of Jesus, I divorce you.
3. I break every marital covenant with the spirit spouse, in the name of Jesus.
4. I destroy every one of your instruments, mirrors, camera, video cameras, cell phones, computers that you are using to monitor me and my progress by fire in the name of Jesus.

5. Every generational covenant, bond, and agreement from my mother's lineage troubling my destiny be destroyed by fire in Jesus name.
6. In the name of Jesus, I release myself, my virtue, my glory, and every gift that God has given to me from the captivity of satanic occurrence in Jesus name
7. I break any soul tie and covenant between me and any of my parents in the name of Jesus.
8. Any power sponsoring the activity of satanic covenants in my family, as I clap my hands and pray, die in the name of Jesus.
9. Any altar that is receiving animal blood, human blood to strengthen satanic bonds against me, scatter by fire in the name of Jesus.

Meditate on this: Are you tired of the presence of a spiritual spouse in your life? Do you want to be free?

Do this: Write out seven reasons why you think you need to be delivered.

Pray this: Father, I come in the name of Jesus, and I declare that I am free from every demonic spouse I am entangled with.

Chapter Ten

DEALING WITH THE SEEDS/OFFSPRING OF DEMON SPOUSE

> *"And I will put enmity between you and the woman, and between your seed and her Seed; He shall bruise him on the heel."*
>
> **Genesis 3:15**

Conception begins with a seed. There's no life without first sowing a seed. From plants to animals to man, there is always a seed before formation and delivery. God created the world with His word-the seed. God refers to His word as a seed. In Mark 4, Jesus mentioned that the word is to the Kingdom as seed is to harvest. He said, *"So is the Kingdom of God as if a man should cast seed into the ground..." (Verse 26a).* Seeds are meant for reproduction, and the kind of seed you sow will determine the fruit you reap.

The Greek word "Sperma" is translated in English as Seed[1]. The seed of man is spermatozoa; the seed of a woman is her offspring, the seed of God is Jesus Christ, and the seed of Christ is the church.

Do you know that Money is also a seed? Enlightenment is a seed. Education is a seed. People plant different seeds and harvest according to how or what they have planted. God's word rightly puts that "what (seed) you sow is what you reap—birth." A mango seed produces mango fruit. A monkey can only birth its kind. Have you ever seen a woman putting birth to a bird? I guess not! This is proof that you can only reproduce the seed you've sown. Now, the same thing applies to demons.

DEMONS ARE REAL!

You may be wondering how demons plant seeds and where they plant them. The truth is, Satan and his demons are real! They are forces that exist in the world today. They have one goal, which is to manipulate people, use them as tools to fulfill the devil's agenda and to make them question their faith in Jesus Christ.

It's important to know that demons have spouses. Demon spouses leave seeds in the body of their victims. How do I know? The Bible says that "*We wrestle not against flesh and blood, but against principalities and powers.*" Life is spiritual, and we have to live in that reality. Because life is

---

[1] https://www.biblestudytools.com/lexicons/greek/nas/sperma.html

spiritual, marriage too is spiritual. Yes, it is! Demons have intercourse with people and plant their seeds in them.

The Bible records the first description of demons and sex in Genesis, where fallen angels and women coupled to birth a race of creatures. It says, *"The children of the supernatural beings who had married these women became famous heroes and warriors. They were called the Nephilim and lived on earth at that time and even later."*

Biblical Archeology Society refers to the **Nephilim,** which means **fallen ones,** as the mysterious beings in Genesis 6:4[2]. They were the product of the intercourse between the divine beings-sons of God and human women.

Today, demons are still out to continue infesting what God has made and thwart the purpose of God for one's life. And they achieve this by implanting a seed so they can produce after their kind. That's why most times when you see people behave in certain manners, you need to know that it's not their true personality. Sometimes, they are empowered by a demon to manifest in that way. Sadly, people get married to demons without knowing. It could be through an oath, covenant, relationship, or just like the Bible reveals in Matthew—the mad man of Gadarene. In truth, demons are real, and they still possess people.

However, God has promised REDEMPTION, and it can be achieved by destroying demonic seeds. But before we know what posture to take to do away with their seeds, it's best to know what the seeds are and their functions.

---

[2] https://www.biblicalarchaeology.org/daily/biblical-topics/hebrew-bible/who-are-the-nephilim/

DEMONIC CHILDREN

First, you must understand that anyone married to a spirit spouse is susceptible to difficulties navigating through their divine path in life. From marriage to business, to living a fulfilled life, nothing seems to work well for them! Apart from torments from the bond, their eyes are blinded to physical relationships. Just as the Bible says that we can't serve two masters at a time, you can't be married to a spirit spouse and successfully marry a spouse in the physical realm, let alone produce children.

When the devil gains entrance into your womb, he pollutes it and renders you inadequate, and leaves you in the lurch. Having demonic children means sinking into the ocean of frustration and desolation because everything about your life will be mysterious. The distress, the discomfort, the dominance, the manipulation, and you will just wish to die!

Demonic seeds don't allow their victims to flourish in what they do. They are always out to hinder the success of every good thing their prey delve into. A story was told of a woman who was possessed by a demonic spirit. Before the possession, she had a beautiful marriage and a thriving business. But, immediately she got possessed, everything went on the blink.

She became violent, both in actions and words. On one occasion, she threatened to leave her husband and later packed her things. Her business started crumbling, and all she'd lived for, in a flash, came to a dead end. Her life became messed up, yet she didn't know what had come over her.

The truth is, except God delivers one from the servitude of the enemy, such a person is heading for destruction. The funny thing is that because the devil wants to have his way and take over the world, he doesn't want to multiply. So, he spreads his seeds in every womb that looks receptive.

Then, because a child must be like their parents, these children manifest like their father—the devil would do. Unfortunately, these seeds are not usually seen with the physical eyes. All their manifestation is in the spirit realm, and that's the most infuriating part of it. Imagine that you saw a demon with your physical eyes. Wouldn't you think of killing such with even your bare hands? The Bible says that the weapons of our warfare are not carnal. That's why you need to be sensitive in the spirit to know when the devil strikes.

As I'd earlier mentioned, these demons don't have anything good to share with humans. So, they are also jealous of women who are on the verge of getting married and will always attack them. They hinder their victims from getting married. That is why some beautiful ladies may not have suitors, and when they have one, their relationship does not end well. The wickedness in the heart of the spirit spouse is to make children in the spirit world suck on women's breasts in their dreams.

This is done to imprison and introduce spiritual union with an individual. The spirit husband/wife may prevent someone from successfully having their marriage or conceive children. Even when one has earthly marriage, they instigate problems and shatter the beauty and purpose of marriage.

They are responsible for chasing all the potential suitors away from women and sometimes use their character flaws against them so that no man admires them no matter how beautiful they are. They eventually veil the woman and make her too small to see to before their potential husbands.

These and more are punishments from a spirit spouse that are meted out to those who give birth or nurse children in the dream. If you are a married woman expecting a child, spirit husbands will introduce spirit children to steal and block the child from being conceived or delivered. Such an act can keep a married woman from having children for the rest of her marriage. May that not be your position, in Yeshua's name.

WHAT ARE THE DREAMS OF SPIRIT SPOUSES AND CHILDREN?

These are the signs that one is being possessed by an evil spirit.

- They Dream of kissing a person
- They Dream of having sex
- They Play with children in the dream
- Back a child in the dream
- They Breastfeed a baby in the dream
- They take a child from someone in the dream
- Losing pregnancy in the dream
- Eating in the dream
- Sucking the breasts of a person in the dream

- Having the feeling that you are being watched by spirit spouse
- Finding yourself pregnant with a child in the dream
- When you see that your wedding gown is torn, disappeared, or stolen in the dream
- One pair of shoes is stolen or missing.
- Finding that you are swimming or walking in the river in the dreamland
- When you see snakes chasing you in the dream
- When you see yourself helping people to birth to their babies at the hospital
- Loss of baby or children in the dream
- Masturbating or having incest in the dream
- Finding yourself in a brothel in a dream
- Purchasing condoms in a dream
- Having sexual dreams with gay or lesbian
- Finding yourself being raped in the dream
- Playing with reproductive organs
- Having an erection in the dream
- When you dream that you have two sexual organs
- When you have an affair with unknown persons in the dream
- Getting married to someone you do not know

HOW TO MARK AND DESTROY THESE DEMONIC SEEDS AND THEIR CHILDREN

The Bible says that the seed of the woman shall destroy the head of the serpent. When Jesus died, he gave us victory over the forces of darkness, sin, and hell. The truth is, the *finished work* was to finish off the devil and sin. Also, Jesus said in Luke 4:18, *"The Spirit of the Lord is upon me because he has anointed me to preach the good news to the poor; He has sent me to announce release to the captives and recovery of sight to the blind, and to send forth as delivered those who are oppressed."* This is why Jesus came to the world. He didn't just come to save us from sin; he came to deliver us as well.

Matthew 1:21 reaffirms this. It says, *"And she shall bring forth a son, and you shall call His name Jesus, for He will save His people from their sins."* In truth, Jesus is the only name for deliverance—both from sin and Satan. And, because Jesus is the deliverer, you can neither be free nor destroy the demons and his seeds without being saved from sin.

KNOW JESUS; GET EQUIPPED

A servant cannot fight his master. The Scripture tells us that no servant is greater than his master. So, if your master is the devil, then he has every right over you. In other words, you're a subject to him, so he can deal with you as he pleases. But, if God is your Master, Satan automatically becomes your subject. You can't be in sin and attempt to fight the devil—your master. He will make your life miserable because you're living at his mercy.

Until you are saved from sin, you remain a slave to the devil. The Bible says that demons tremble at the mention of the name of Jesus. And, you can't call on that name if you don't believe in it. Mark 16:17a says, *"And these signs will accompany those who believe in my name: in my name, they will cast out demons."* So, if you don't believe you can't destroy!

How do you believe? By accepting Jesus into your life. Jesus says in Revelation 3: 20, *"Behold I stand at the door and knock, if any man hears my voice and open the door, I will come in to him and sup with him, and he with me."* What are you still waiting for?

GUARD YOUR HEART!

Now that you are saved, you must guard your heart with all diligence, so you don't fall back into the trap of the enemy. Satan is not happy when someone repents from his/her sin. He's always out to ensure that he takes them to himself. So, he does this by bringing up enticing engagements, interactions, and even associations, to have you back. That's why you must be sensitive and watchful, so he doesn't get you.

Meditate on this: God has given us a name above every other name, which is Jesus. At the name of Jesus, every knee bows, and every tongue confesses that Jesus is Lord. Jesus is all you need to demolish the activities of the devil and his demons. Do you know Jesus?

Do this: Examine your life and dreams and see if there is any connection between you and any strange entity.

Pray this: Father, in the name of Jesus! I pray that every ungodly tie in my life is broken in Jesus' name.

Make these declarations in prayer against the demon spouse offspring's

1. Every spiritual child attached to my life, I bind and cast you out, in the name of Jesus.
2. I refuse to be established by demonic children, in the name of Jesus.
3. I destroy the power of any demonic child in my life, in the name of Jesus.
4. Every link between any spiritual child and me, be broken now, in the name of Jesus.
5. Let all spirit children attached to my life be electrocuted, in the name of Jesus.
6. Any demonic child claiming me as their mother/father, perish by fire, in the name of Jesus.
7. Blood of Jesus, silence all spiritual children crying against me, in Jesus' name.
8. I bring the blood of the Lord over every spiritual child now, in Jesus' name.
9. I refuse and reject the ancestral covenant with any spiritual child, in Jesus' name.
10. I arrest you spiritual children and I command you to die, in Jesus' name.
11. I break the power of spirit children over every department of my life, in the name of Jesus.
12. Every spirit child in my life, gather yourselves together, collapse and perish, in Jesus' name.
13. Lion of Judah eat up every spirit child attached to my life, in the name of Jesus.

14. Every masquerading spiritual child working against me summersault and perish, in the name of Jesus.
15. I destroy the power of the spiritual children in my life, in the name of Jesus.
16. O Lord let your arrow be strong and pierce unto the hearts of my spirit children, in Jesus' name.
17. I plead the blood of Jesus against every spiritual child, in the name of Jesus.
18. All you spiritual children affecting my life be chained unto death, in the name of Jesus.
19. Any spirit child drawing me away from God, die, in Jesus' name.
20. You the spirit children in my life, enter inside the dustbin of fire now, in the name of Jesus

Chapter Eleven

HOW TO ESTABLISH COVENANT WITH GOD

*And I, behold, I establish my covenant
with you, and with your seed after you;*
Genesis 9:1

According to the Bible, there are seven covenants, four of which God made with the nation of Israel. They are; the Abrahamic, Palestinian, Mosaic, and the Davidic covenant. Three of these covenants are unconditional. This means they do not depend on the obedience or disobedience of the children of Israel to be fulfilled. God fully establishes His covenants and sticks with it.

The Mosaic covenant, however, is conditional. It completely demands the allegiance of the children of Israel for it be favorable to them. Otherwise, they will partake of the curses. The Adamic, Noahic, and the new covenants were established between God and mankind generally. Unlike the Mosaic law, these are not limited to the children of Israel.

> *Now the Lord has said unto Abram, Get thee out of the country, and from thy kindred, and thy father's house, unto a land that I will show thee. And I will make of thee a great nation, and I will bless thee, and make thy name great, and thou shalt be a blessing: and I will bless them that bless thee, and curse him that curseth thee: and in thee shall all families of the earth be blessed.*
>
> **Genesis 12:1-3**

The Adamic Covenant can be further referred to as the Covenant in Eden (covenant of grace) (Genesis 3:16-19). This covenant made in the garden of Eden showed the responsibility of man to the creation and the directive of God to man with respect to the tree of the knowledge of good and evil. The Adamic Covenant included the curses pronounced against mankind for the sin of Adam and Eve. (Genesis, 3:15).

The Noahic Covenant is in two parts. On one end, it was established by God with Noah. On the other end, God made it as a covenant to all of humanity. It is an unconditional covenant. Right after the flood, God made a promise to Noah that He would not destroy life on the earth again with a flood (see Genesis chapter 9). This made God give a rainbow which was a sign of the covenant. This sealed the promise from God to man to not destroy the entire earth with a flood and a reminder that God can and will judge sin.

Abrahamic Covenant (Genesis 12: 1-3, 6-7; 13:14-17; 17:1-14; 22:15-18).

In the Abrahamic covenant, God gave Abraham quite a number of promises. He promised to make his name great (Genesis 12:2), He promised him great descendants whose numbers cannot be counted (Genesis 13:16), and He also promised to make him the father of nations (Genesis 174-5). Moving on, God spoke to him about the kind of people that shall come out of his loins. He gave him a full breakdown of the nation of Israel, which will come out of Abraham's seed. The facts of the Abrahamic covenant is laid out in several places in the book of Genesis (12:7; 13:14-15; 15:18-21). Another very important aspect of the Abrahamic is the saying, *"In thee shall all nations of the earth be blessed."* (Genesis 12:3, 22:18). Now, we understand that beyond material blessings, this is a reference to the Messiah, who would come from the line of Abraham.

> *And it shall come to pass, when all these things are come upon thee, the blessing and the curse, which I have set before thee, the blessing and the curse, which I have set before thee, and thou shalt call them to mind among all the nations, wither the Lord thy God hath driven thee, and shalt return unto the Lord thy God, and shalt obey his voice according to all that I command thee this day, thou and thy children, with all thine heart, and with all thy soul; that then the LORD thy God will turn thy captivity, and have compassion upon thee, and*

will return and gather thee from all the nations, wither the LORD thy God hath scattered thee. If any of thine be driven out unto the outmost parts of heaven, from thence will the LORD thy God gather thee, and from thence will he fetch thee: and the Lord thy God will bring thee into the land which thy fathers possessed, and though shalt possess it; and he will do thee good, and multiply thee above thy fathers. And the Lord thy God will circumcise thine heart, and the heart of thy seed, to love the Lord thy God with all thine heart, and with all thy soul, that thou mayest live. And the Lord thy God will put all these curses upon thine enemies, and on them, that hate thee, which persecuted thee. And thou shalt return and obey the voice of the Lord and do all his commandments which I command thee this day. And the Lord thy God will make thee plenteous in every work of thine hand, in the fruit of thy body, and in the fruit of thy cattle, and in the fruit of thy land, for good: for the Lord will again rejoice over thee for good, as he rejoiced over thy fathers; if thou shalt hearken unto the voice of the Lord thy God, to keep his commandments and his statutes which are written in his book of the law, and if though turn unto the Lord thy God all thine heart, and with all thy soul.

Deuteronomy 30:1-10

Palestinian covenant (Deuteronomy 30:1-10)

The Palestinian Covenant, which can be referred to as Land Covenant, amplifies the land aspect that was exhaustive in the Abrahamic Covenant. According to the terms of this type, if the people disobeyed, God would scatter around the world (Deuteronomy 30:3-4), but eventually, He would restore the nation (verse 5). And whenever there is a restoration of the nation, they will obey Him perfectly (verse 8), and God will make them prosper (verse 9).

The Mosaic Covenant:

This contains the various laws and ordinances God delivered to Moses for the children of Israel. It either invoked God's blessing or punishment on the people. It all depended on how they responded. Part of this covenant was the Ten Commandments (Exodus 20), and the other Laws, which contained over 600 commands – roughly 300 are positive and the other 300 negative. The history books of the Old Testament (Joshua –Esther) gave a detailed history of how the children of Israel, on several occasions, obeyed God's commands and reaped the rewards and other times when they disobeyed, and they were severely punished. The scriptures below detail the blessing and cursing.

> *Behold, I set before you this day a blessing and a curse; a blessing, if ye obey the commandments of the LORD your God, which I command you*

this day: and a curse, if ye will not obey the commandments of the LORD your God, but turn aside out of the way which I command you this day, to go after other gods, which ye have not known. And it shall come to pass when the Lord thy God hath brought thee in unto the land whither thou goest to possess it, that thou shalt put the blessing upon mount Gerizim, and the curse upon mount Ebal.

Deuteronomy 11:26-29

Davidic Covenant

(2 Samuel 7:8-16). Kind David was famously known as a man after God's heart. The promise of God to Abraham and his seed would be carried on and established through the line of David. God gave David an eternal promise that his seed would reign on the throne forever. Of course, God wasn't just talking about the throne in Jerusalem; rather, He referred to the throne of Christ in heaven. David caught a glimpse of this by revelation when he wrote, *"...the LORD hath said unto my Lord, Sit at my right hand till make thine enemies thine footstool" (Psalm 110:1).* This future king was Jesus Christ, who lives now and forever (Luke 1:32-33).

Now therefore so shalt though say unto my servant David, thus saith the Lord of hosts, I took thee from the sheepcote, from following the sheep, to be ruler over my people, over Israel: and I was with thee whithersoever thou wentest, and have cut off all thine enemies out of thy sight, and have made thee a great name, like unto the name of the great men that are in the earth. Moreover, I will appoint a place for my people Israel, and will plant them, that they may dwell in a place of their own, and move no more; neither shall the children of wickedness afflict them anymore. as beforetime, and as since the time that I commanded judges to be over my people Israel, and have caused thee to rest from all thine enemies. Also, the Lord telleth thee that ne will make thee a house. And when thy days be fulfilled, and thou shalt sleep with thy fathers, I will set up thy seed after thee, which shall proceed out of thy bowels, and I will establish his kingdom. He shall build a house for my name, and I will establish the throne of his kingdom forever. I will be his father, and he shall be my son. If he commits iniquity, I will chasten him with the rod of men, and with the stripes of the children of men; but my mercy shall not depart away from him, as I took it from Saul, Whom I put away before thee. And thine house and thy kingdom shall be established forever before thee: thy throne shall be established forever.

2 Samuel 7:8-16

New Covenant (Jeremiah 31:31-34).

The New Covenant is God's all-time solution for the problem of mankind. Every other covenant mentioned and treated as a shadow of this covenant. God started painting the picture of His ultimate plan right from the garden of Eden, and in the fullness of time, He revealed it through Jesus. All the other covenants were weak, but they were sufficient for their times. The new covenant was God's ace in the hole. Now that we're under the new covenant, both Jews and Gentiles are free from the penalty of the Law. Now, we have received salvation as a free gift (Ephesians 2:8-9).

> *Behold, the days come, saith the Lord, that I will make a new covenant with the house of Israel, and with the house of Judah: not according to the covenant that I made with their fathers in the day that I took them by the hand to bring them out of the land of Egypt; which my covenant they brake, although I was an husband unto them. Saith the Lord: but this shall be the covenant that I will make with the house of Israel; after those days, saith the Lord, I will put my law in their inward parts, and write it in their hearts; and will be their God, and they shall be my people. And they shall teach no more every man his neighbor, and every man his brother, saying, know the Lord: for they shall all know me from the least of them unto the greatest*

*of them, saith the Lord: for I will forgive their
iniquity, and I will remember their sin no more.*
Jeremiah 3:31-34

Meditate on this: God was so meticulous in laying out His covenant with His people. Have you ever thought maybe He had it all planned out?

Do this: Pick your Bible and search out the promises of God to you. Read them out loud to yourself.

Pray this: Dear God, I thank You for Your covenant of life and peace in my life. I pray that the reality of Your grace will not be frustrated in my life. Amen

Chapter Twelve

FINDING AND CHOOSING A GODLY SPOUSE

(Amos 3:3, Genesis 24:3-4, Psalms 37:4)

The subject of finding and choosing a Godly spouse is of extreme importance. And the choice of one's marital spouse goes a long way to determine the lives of the individuals involved. As a result of this, the choice of a spouse is one of the greatest decisions an individual has to make. How then does one find a Godly partner? Can a person just choose anyone he's attracted to? Or is his partner just going to walk up to him and say, "Hey! I'm your spouse?" It does not work this way. Most of what we see on TV programs and films are simply fictitious, and it's not applicable to real life.

Why do you need to find a Godly spouse? Here is what King Solomon has to say: *"You may inherit all you own from your parents, but a sensible wife is a gift from the LORD. (Prov. 19:14).* He reveals that a sensible wife is gotten from the Lord.

You have got to take deliberate steps in the right direction to ensure you're not on the wrong side of the track. The Bible gives us some pointers as to how this can be achieved. The first point to consider is that whoever you will be selecting as your spouse must be someone you can easily relate with. He or she must be Godly. The scripture says;

> *Can two walk together, except they be agreed?*
> **Amos 3:3**

Life itself is an agreement. You must, as a child of God, be intent on marrying a spouse who is a believer as well. This will save you a lot of trouble and stress. This already narrows down your options. Now you know you can't marry just anybody. Neither can you be yoked with unbelievers (2 Corinthians 6:14).

We see a good illustration of this demonstrated by Abraham. At the time when he was to choose a wife for his son, Isaac, he gave the servant whom he sent a strict warning *"you shall not take a wife unto my son of the daughters of the Canaanites…"*. We can relate the daughters of the Canaanites in Abraham's day to the daughters of the world – unbelievers in our present age. This is a compromise you cannot afford to make!

> *And I will make thee swear by the LORD, the*
> *God of heaven, and the God of earth, that*
> *thou shalt not take a wife unto my son of the*

> *daughters of the Canaanites, among whom I
> dwell: but thou shalt go unto my country, and to
> my kindred, and take a wife unto my son Isaac.*
> **Genesis 24:3-4**

As someone who is born again, you should delight yourself in the LORD. Abraham made his servant to swear by the God of heaven that even if the only option left was to pick a woman from the daughters of the Canaanites; he should rather not pick a wife for his son.

Scripture goes further to tell us that "when you delight yourself in the Lord, He will give you the desires of your heart." This includes a Godly spouse. This is how scripture puts it;

> *Delight thyself also in the Lord: and he shall
> give thee the desires of thine heart.*
> **Psalms 37:4**

Note: acts such as fornication destroys the sanctity of marriage. Do not commit fornication! It is a sin, and God will judge you for that.

There are a number of ways you can find and choose a Godly spouse. One of such ways include;

PETITION

What is a petition?

A petition is a written prayer, which acts almost like a legal document. The use of a petition is a very effective form of prayer and warfare. Through the petition, many people entreat God for their spouse. Therefore, a petition is a legal form of prayer and should be the first step that one should take when looking for a Godly spouse. In Hebrew, the word petition is described in three words (SHELAH, MISHALAH, AND BAGGA SHAH)[3]. The words have the meaning of "to ask, beg, borrow, lay to charge, consult, demand, desire earnestly, inquire, pray, request, petition, or wish.

> *And if ye go to war in your land against the enemy that oppresseth you, then ye shall **blow an alarm with the trumpets;** and ye shall be remembered before the LORD your God, and ye shall be saved from your enemies.*
>
> **Numbers 10:9**

From the above scripture, it is sensible to say that our petition should start with the declaration of who God is. Exalt and eulogize Him; Our God is the Almighty, creator of the universe, the God of Abraham, Isaac, and Israel. He can measure the waters in the hollow of His hand, mark off the heavens with the span of His hand, gather the dust of the Earth in a measure, weigh the mountains and hill on a balance (Isaiah 40: 12). This declaration is like a trumpet call in the heaven. We would state the legal grounds we stand on. Our faith in the covenant promise of God through the blood of Jesus.

---

[3] https://pdf4pro.com/amp/view/petitions-english-kanaan-ministries-40c391.html

After the declaration, the next thing to do is to state your request. The Bible says, *"... make your requests known to God" (Phil. 4:6)*. In this case, it can be marriage, children, the salvation of a loved one, protection, finances, spiritual breakthrough, and growth, for memories to surface, or any uproot anything that threatens God's fullness and peace in our lives.

Then, you go on to sign the petition and get someone to stand in agreement with you. Declare the petition sealed with the blood of the Lamb. Ensure you note the date to establish the petition in the heavens, the earth, the waters, and under the earth.

The following are some of the scriptures that are based on some common petitions;

Marriage (1Corinthians 7:13 - 14)

Loved ones to be saved (Judges 23, 2nd Peter 3:9)

Safety and Protection (Psalms 91, Jeremiah 15:20 -21)

Memories to surface (Luke 12: 2 – 3, Exodus 23:29 – 30)

The promise of God to you is this:

Verily I say unto you, whatsoever ye shall bind on earth shall be bound in heaven: and whatsoever ye shall loose on earth shall be loosed in heaven. Again I say unto you, that if two of you shall agree on earth as touching anything that they shall ask, it shall be done for them of my father in heaven. For where two or three are gathered together in my name, there am I in the midst of them.
Matthew 18:18-20

Hannah made a petition, and her desire was to have a child, and God granted her request. To petition your request to God, your soul must be poured out to the lord. The favor of the Lord comes to those who cry from their heart.

> *And she vowed a vow, and said, O LORD of hosts, if thou wilt indeed look on the affliction of thine handmaid, and remember me, and not forget thine handmaid, but wilt give unto thine handmaid a man child, then I will give him unto the LORD all the days of his life, and there shall no razor come upon his head. And it came to pass, as she continued praying before the LORD, that Eli marked her mouth. But Hannah went not up; for she said unto her husband, I will not go up until the child be weaned, and then I will bring him, that he may appear before the LORD, and there abide forever.*
>
> **1Samuel 1:11-12, 22**

> *When he maketh inquisition for blood, he remembered them: he forgetteth not the cry of the humble.*
>
> **Psalms 9:12**

Your petition must be poured out in tears.

Grant thee according to thine own heart, and fulfill all they counsel. We will rejoice in thy salvation,

CONQUER SPIRITUAL SPOUSES

and in the name of our God, we will set up our banners: the LORD fulfill all thy petitions.

Psalms 20:4

It is advisable to write out a petition in whatever you believe in and pour your heart out to Him.

And Adonijah, the son of Haggith, came to Bathsheba, the mother of Solomon. And she said, Cometh thou peaceably? And he said, peaceably. He said; moreover, I have somewhat to say unto thee. And she said, Say on. And he said, Thou knowest that the kingdom was mine, and that all Israel set their faces on me, that I should reign: howbeit the kingdom is turned about, and is become my brother's: for it was his from the LORD. And now I ask one petition of thee, deny me not. And she said unto him, say on. And he said, speak, I pray thee, unto Solomon the king, (for he will not say thee nay,) that he give me Abishag the Shunammite to wife. And Bathsheba said, well; I will speak for thee unto the king.

1Kings 2:13-18

And the king said again unto Esther on the second day at the banquet of wine, what is thy petition, Queen Esther? And it shall be granted thee: and what is they request? And it shall be performed, even to the half of the kingdom. Then, Esther, the queen answered and said, if

> *I have found favor in thy sight, O king, and if*
> *it pleases the king, let my life be given me at*
> *my petition, and my people at my request:*
> **Esther 7:2-3**

Go to God in prayer and declare who He is to you. This declaration is like blowing a trumpet call in heaven.

Scriptures that can help you in a petition for a Godly spouse.

> *Marriage is honorable in all, and the bed undefiled:*
> *but whoremongers and adulterers God will judge.*
> **Hebrews 13:4**

> *And the woman which hath a husband that*
> *believeth not, and if he be pleased to dwell with her*
> *let her not leave him. For the unbelieving husband*
> *is sanctified by the wife, and the unbelieving*
> *wife is sanctified by the husband: else were your*
> *children unclean, but now are they holy.*
> **1Corinthians 7:13-14**

Be committed to God and His purpose

Another point to consider in choosing a Godly spouse is to ensure that you are committed to God and His purposes. We can see this in Abraham's instructions to his servant.

Abraham's heart was wholly set on keeping the promises of God.

> *But thou shalt go unto my country, and to my kindred, and take a wife unto my son Isaac. And the servant said unto him, Peradventure, the woman, will not be willing to follow me unto this land: must I needs bring thy son again unto the land from whence thou camest? And Abraham said unto him, Beware thou that thou bring not my son thither again. The LORD God of heaven, which took me from my father's house, and from the land of my kindred, and which spake unto me, and that sware unto me, saying, Unto thy seed will I give this land; he shall send his angel before thee, and thou shalt take a wife unto my son from thence. And if the woman will not be willing to follow thee, then thou shalt be clear from this my oath: only bring not my son thither again.*
> **Genesis 24:4-8(KJV)**

Like Abraham, when you're seeking a Godly mate, God's purposes and His will must be your anchor and guide. When this is in place, you can rest assured that you will get God's very best for you.

Meditate on this: How did you get your spouse? Was it inspired by the Holy Spirit or directed by your flesh? If you're single, how are you going about your search?

Do this: Examine your life and your home. List out the signs that reveal that God is present in your home and marriage.

Pray this: Lord, I pray that You deliver me from the consequences of any wrong step that I might have taken in time past in the choice of choosing a life partner. Do not let my mistake bring destiny-altering situation in my life.

Chapter Thirteen

DELIVERANCE PRAYERS AGAINST EVIL MARITAL ATTRACTIONS OR STRANGE WOMEN/MEN

"Wherefore they are no more twain but one flesh. What therefore God has joined together let no man put asunder."
Matthew 19:6

It is the will of God that a man and his wife should live together in love and unity for a lifetime. The marriage covenant is not be broken for any reason. God's original plan is that only death should separate a couple. However, there are many forces that seek to destroy marriage. These forces can be called anti-marriage forces. They operate by planting evil marital magnets in the home. Such magnets include activities of strange men/women, promiscuity by either partner, 'Jezebel' activities, anger and control by ungodly in-laws. If you are experiencing any of these events, it is time to roll up your sleeves, fight for your marriage and stop the activities of satanic intruders or strange women and men into your marriage [Job 11: 4-20]. As you open your heart, may the Holy Ghost fire purge out every evil marital magnet designed by the enemy to ruin your marriage. Pray these prayer points with holy madness. As long as the marriage is legitimately structured, meaning neither party is liable for the sin of adultery (re-marrying while the first partner is still alive), God will fight for you.

JEREMIAH. 1:10: See, I have this day set thee over the nations and over the kingdoms, to root out, and pull down, and to destroy, and to throw down, to build, and to plant. GEN. 1:26 And God said, let us make man in our image, after our likeness: and let them have dominion over the fish of the sea and over the fowl of the air, and over the cattle, and over all the earth, and over every creeping thing the creepeth upon the earth.

GENESIS. 3:15 And I will put enmity between thee and the woman, and between thy seed and her seed; it shall bruise they head, and thou shalt bruise his heel.

LUKE 10:19 Behold, I give unto you power to tread on serpents and scorpions, and over all the power of the enemy: and nothing shall by any means hurt you.

REV 12:9-10: And the great dragon was cast out, that old serpent, called the devil, and satan, which deceiveth the whole world: he was cast over into the earth, and his angels were cast out with him. And I heard a loud voice saying in heaven, now is come salvation, and strength, and the kingdom of our God, and the power of His Christ: for the accuser of our brethren is cast down, which accused them before our God day and night.

CONFESSIONS

With my whole heart I believe the Most High God. I believe His Word and I confess with my mouth that He is Jehovah God who created the heavens and the Earth. I confess that He is the beginning and the end of all things. He was, He is and forever shall be. With God, I believe nothing is impossible, God has spoken once and twice I have heard this that all power in heaven and Earth belongs to Him.

As I say this power and confess the word of God, I command all the spirits of distractions and hindrances to be bound, in the name of Jesus. I cast away from me every spirit of tiredness, weakness and defeat. In the mighty name of Jesus Christ, I command every knee of things in heaven, on Earth and in the seas that are against this prayer to kneel and be bound.

I ask for the presence of God to overshadow me with the fire of the Holy Spirit and His anointing. Let the anointing that breaks yokes fall upon my head now and run through me to bring in great deliverance. As it is written, it shall come to pass today that the burden of the spirit husband/wife [shall] be taken off my shoulders and his/her yoke off my neck and the yoke shall be destroyed by the reason of the anointing.

By the grace of God, I have accepted Jesus Christ and I am now saved. Jesus has redeemed me- He shed his blood for me, washed me in that same blood and brought me back from the hand of my strong enemy; He loves me. I declare that I am a beneficiary of every work of redemption and restoration which Jesus finished on the cross of Calvary. Through the death and resurrection of Jesus victory is established over the power of death. Now, I shall not die but live because Jesus has become my deliverer, my defender, my protector, my high tower, my refuge, my victory, and the author and the finisher of my faith. Jesus has set me free; I now accept deliverance. I declare that I am delivered from the law of sin and death. God has translated my life from the kingdom of darkness into the kingdom of his dear own son, the kingdom of life and light.

I announce that all power in heaven and on Earth belongs to my Lord Jesus. Jesus Christ has given me authority in His name against all powers of darkness and their operations. Therefore now, in the name of Jesus, I overcome you spirit husband/wife by the blood of Jesus. I am born of the Most High God and I have overcome the world by my faith.

I am a child of light; darkness cannot overcome or comprehend me. I command all forces and entities of spiritual marriage fashioned against me to be struck with the light of God. Light and darkness cannot dwell together. I use the Word of God as my light to break the spell of the spirit husband/ wife oppressing me through darkness.

In the name of Jesus Christ, I reject and break every conscious/ unconscious link with every spirit husband/wife formed against me through my bloodline, dreams, food, gifts, or by any unlawful means. It is written, "Every tree that my Heavenly Father did not plant shall be rooted up" [Mathew 15:13]. I am bought out of bondage with a price. Jesus paid the price through His shed blood. It is recorded in His Word that God predestined me to belong to Him before the foundations of the world were laid. Furthermore, it is written that my "Maker is my husband; the Lord of Hosts is His name; and my Redeemer the Holy one of Israel; The God of the Whole Earth shall He be called" [Isiah 54: 5]. It is also recorded that whosoever defiles the temple of God shall be destroyed. I therefore command destruction upon the spirit husband/ wife that has been stubbornly defiling me, the temple of God now!

In the name of Jesus, I use the Blood of the Lamb of God and I nullify the effect of every spiritual dowry ever paid on my life to every spirit husband. Let every legal ground in the form of agreement, promises, vows and covenants made by me consciously or unconsciously, or made on my behalf be passed away now; behold all things have become new. I renounce and I reject every white stone and every object given to me by the spirit husband/ wife. I bind and I cast out to the bottomless pit every evil spirit transferred into me through my contact with the spirit husband/wife physically or in my dreams. I break every rule and law binding me to the spirit husband/ wife with the blood of Jesus. I set on fire every wedding certificate, wedding ring, gown, gifts and every other ornament in the name of Jesus. Let every spirit child that is between us roast now, in the name of Jesus. I release the blood of Jesus to purge my body and cleanse me of every sexual pollution and contamination of the spirit husband/ wife.

Every covenant that is strongly binding me to any evil spiritual marriage be broken now. For it is written, God has made a new covenant with me and all others are old and disannulled. Every curse place upon my body, my business, my property, my home and marriage by the sprit husband/ wife loose your hold now by the blood of Jesus. Who shall curse him that the Lord has blessed? It is written, God will bless them that bless me and curse them that curse me.

Whosoever rolls a stone, it shall fall on him; and whosoever dug a pit shall fall therein. Therefore, I return to the senders all curses placed upon me and anything that pertains to me, in the name of Jesus 777-fold. Every tongue revolting against me in the kingdom of darkness, I condemn you with the written judgment of God.

I hereby declare that there is no divination or enchantment against me. It is written that "surely there is no enchantment against Jacob, neither is there any divination against Israel; according to this time it shall be said of Jacob and Israel, what hath God wrought!" [Numbers 23:23]. Let every physical and spiritual activities of land and marine witchcraft be completely wiped off now by the blood of Jesus.

Let every water associated activities of spiritual husband/wife in my dreams be polluted with the blood of Jesus. Let the fire of God destroy every workmanship of the devil fashioned against me through the operations of the spirit husband/wife now. Every attack and operations of the demons of spiritual marriages launched through eating in the dream, become impotent and of no effect now. I stand in the faith of Christ as it is written I shall eat a deadly thing and it shall not harm me.

In the name of Jesus, I use the blood of Jesus to set a boundary between me and the spirit husband/wife. Henceforth let no spirit husband/wife trouble me for I bear in my body the mark of the precious blood of the Lamb of God. I command that the spirit husband/wife cannot steal, or kill, or destroy any good thing in my life any longer. God has raised me up to sit with Jesus Christ in heavenly places, far above principalities, powers, dominions and all their thrones and kingdoms whether visible or invisible. Jesus is the head of all principalities and powers, and I am complete in him who is the head of all things. All the powers of darkness are under my feet. I use the power in the blood and in the name of Jesus to put a stop to all disturbances and oppression in my dreams now. I forbid all forms of sexual attacks, eating, drinking, swimming, wandering, being naked or bathing in my dreams. I shall be far from oppression and from terror, for it shall not come near me. I will both lay me down in peace, and sleep for the Lord only makes me to dwell in safety. Therefore, I shall not fear the powers of the night.

I prophesy to my life that every good thing that the spirit husband/wife has chased away or diverted from reaching me shall be restored. Everything stolen, killed or destroyed shall come back to life, for the Son of Man has come to restore what the locust, cankerworm, palmerworm and the caterpillar have eaten and destroyed. Therefore, I confess and receive divine restoration in my marriage, in my physical, mental and emotional health, in my finances, in my spiritual well-being and in all other areas of my life.

I confess and in the name of Jesus I possess my total deliverance from the bondage of the spirit husband/wife, and I seal my divine freedom with the blood of Jesus.

Prayer Arrows

1. Thank God because he is going to intervene in your marriage through these prayer points.
2. Declare: I destroy anything that is going to stand between me and my prayers now, in the name of Jesus.
3. The anointing to pray to the point of breakthrough in my marriage, fall upon me now, in the name of Jesus.
4. Lord Jesus, I invite you to come to my aid in every difficult situation in my marriage.

5. All my matrimonial properties, which the strange woman sat upon, I withdraw them, in the name of Jesus.
6. I withdraw peace, harmony, unity, love affair between my husband and the strange woman, in the name of Jesus.
7. Lord Jesus, let the strange and unholy love affair between my husband and the strange woman die.
8. I withdraw the favor of my husband from the strange woman, in the name of Jesus.
9. I stand against every power of polygamy, in the name of Jesus.
10. All evil spiritual arrows fired from the strange woman presently in my marriage, loose your grip upon my marriage and go back to your sender, in the name of Jesus.
11. Let confusion be the lot of every strange woman militating against my marriage.
12. Let irreparable division be between... (mention the name of your husband) ... (mention the name of the strange woman if you know it), in the name of Jesus.
13. Angel of God, go right away and disconnect the relationship between my husband and the strange woman, in Jesus' name.
14. Every strange woman militating against my marriage, receive the judgment of God, in the name of Jesus.
15. I nullify every evil judgment that is against me in my marriage, in the name of Jesus.

16. Let all the hindrances to the manifestation of my restoration to my rightful home depart from me and my marriage, in Jesus' name.
17. Lion of Judah consume every fake lion of the strange woman roaring against my marriage, in the name of Jesus.
18. Thunder and fire of God, begin to scatter to pieces, every stronghold of the strange woman in the heart of my husband, in Jesus' name.
19. You demons energizing the relationship between my husband and any strange woman, be rendered impotent and be roasted by the fire of God, in the name of Jesus,
20. Angels of the living God brush off the love of the strange woman completely from the heart of my husband, in Jesus' name.
21. Lord Jesus, create a new heart in my husband by the power in the blood.
22. Every open door that the strange woman is using to gain ground in my husband's life and in my home, receive the blood of Jesus and be closed, in the name of Jesus.
23. God of new beginnings begin a new thing in my marital life, in the name of Jesus.
24. Blood of the Lamb, flow into the foundation of my marital life and give it a new lease of life, in the name of Jesus.
25. Father Lord let your kingdom be established in my marriage, in the name of Jesus.

26. O Lord create a wall of fire between my husband and the strange woman, so that they may be separated forever.
27. Every evil veil covering the face of my husband, receive the fire of God; and burn to ashes, in Jesus mighty name.
28. I recover all my legal rights as the woman of the house from the hands of the strange woman, in the name of Jesus.
29. Every trap of destruction fashioned against my husband by the strange woman, fail woefully, in the name of Jesus.
30. Let the stones of the fire of God locate the heads of my household serpents, in the name of Jesus.
31. I crush the head of the ancient serpent afflicting me and my household with the shoes of iron, in the name of Jesus.
32. Let all the strong holds of the serpent and scorpion in my household receive the thunder of God and be dismantled, in the name of Jesus.
33. Let all habitations of the serpent and the scorpion in my household become utterly desolate, in the name of Jesus.
34. Let the thunder and fire of God, expose all the secret places of my household enemies and consume them all, in the name of Jesus.
35. Let every legal ground of household wickedness in my home be nullified by the blood of Jesus.

36. Let every evil association of the serpent with any member of my family, be terminated now, in the name of Jesus.
37. Let the custodian of my household serpent and scorpion fall down and die, in the name of Jesus.
38. I dismantle the head of all my Goliaths, in the name of Jesus.
39. Every power and spirit in the likeness of snakes attacking me in my dreams be buried, in the name of Jesus.
40. Every property of the enemy in any area of life, receive the fire of God and be melted, in the name of Jesus.
41. I challenge the root of any serpentine spirit deposited in my body to be destroyed by the fire of God, in the name of Jesus.
42. I vomit every poison of the serpent and scorpion circulating in my body, in the name of Jesus.
43. Every serpentine pollution affecting my health be flushed out of my system by the blood of Jesus.
44. Every injury inflicted on my marriage by household serpents, be healed by the blood of Jesus.
45. Every household serpent spitting on my breakthroughs, be neutralized by the blood of Jesus.
46. Every good thing in my life swallowed by the household serpent be converted to fire and vomited into my hands, in Jesus' name.

47. Every good thing in my life paralyzed by the poison of the household serpent, receive the blood of the Lamb and be made whole now, in the name of Jesus.
48. Let all the activities of the serpent in every area of my life be totally paralyzed, in the name of Jesus.
49. Henceforth, let no enemy trouble me for I bear in my body the mark of the blood of the Lamb of God.
50. Father Lord, I thank you for restoring the joy of my marriage in the name of Jesus.

21 DAYS PRAYERS TO CONQUER THE SPIRITUAL SPOUSES

Prayer for Protection:

Father in Heaven, in the name of Jesus Christ, I ask you to forgive me of all my sins I've committed against you and against those made in your image. Lord God Almighty, according to your Word in Psalm 34:7, which says, "The angel of the Lord encamps around those who fear Him and he delivers them.", I ask that you camp your angels around me and around my family members to protect us and keep us safe against demonic attacks and retaliation of the Devil and his demons. I declare Isaiah 54:17, No weapon formed against us shall prosper. No witchcraft nor retaliation formed against us shall prosper. In the name of Jesus Christ, my Savior.

Prayer Points:

1. Spirit spouse, release me by fire, in the name of Jesus.
2. Every spirit spouse, I divorce you by the blood of Jesus.
3. Every spirit wife/every spirit husband, die, in the name of Jesus.
4. Everything you have deposited in my life, come out by fire, in the name of Jesus.
5. Every power that is working against my marriage, fall down and die, in the name of Jesus.
6. I divorce and renounce my marriage with the spirit spouse, in the name of Jesus.
7. I break all covenants entered into with the spirit spouse, in the name of Jesus.
8. I command the thunder fire of God to burn to ashes the wedding gown, ring, photographs and all other materials used for the marriage, in Jesus name.
9. I send the fire of God to burn to ashes the marriage certificate, in the name of Jesus.
10. I break every blood and soul-tie covenants with the spirit spouse in the name of Jesus.
11. I send thunder fire of God to burn to ashes the children born to the marriage, in Jesus' name.
12. I withdraw my blood, sperm or any other part of my body deposited on the altar of the spirit husband or wife, in Jesus name.
13. You spirit spouse tormenting my life and earthly marriage I bind you with hot chains and fetters of

God and cast you out of my life into the deep pit, and I command you not to ever come into my life again, in the name of Jesus.

14. I return to you, every property of yours in my possession in the spirit world, including the dowry and whatsoever was used for the marriage and covenants, in the name of Jesus.
15. I drain myself of all evil materials deposited in my body as a result of our sexual relation, in Jesus name.
16. Lord, send Holy Ghost fire into my root and burn out all unclean things deposited in it by the spirit husband or wife, in the name of Jesus.
17. I break the head of the snake, deposited into my body by the spirit spouse to do me harm, and command it to come out, in the name of Jesus.
18. I purge out, with the blood of Jesus, every evil material deposited in my womb to prevent me from having children on earth.
19. Lord, repair and restore every damage done to any part of my body and my earthly marriage by the spirit spouse, in the name of Jesus.
20. I reject and cancel every curse, evil pronouncement, spell, jinx, enchantment and incantation place upon me by the spirit spouse, in the name of Jesus.
21. I take back and possess all my earthly belonging in the custody of the spirit spouse in Jesus name.
22. I command the spirit spouse to turn his or her back on me forever, in Jesus name.

23. I renounce and reject the name given to me by the spirit spouse, in the name of Jesus.
24. I hereby declare and confess that the Lord Jesus Christ is my Husband for eternity, in Jesus name.
25. I soak myself in the blood of Jesus and cancel the evil mark or writings placed on me, in Jesus name.
26. I set myself free from the stronghold, domineering power and bondage of the spirit husband or wife, in the name of Jesus.
27. I paralyze the remote-control power and work used to destabilize my earthly marriage and to hind me from bearing children for my earthly spouse, in the name of Jesus.
28. I announce to the heavens that I am forever married to Jesus.
29. Every trademark of evil marriage, be shaken out of my life, in the name of Jesus.
30. Every evil writing, engraved by iron pen, be wiped off by the blood of Jesus.
31. I bring the blood of Jesus upon the spirit that does not want to go, in the name of
32. Jesus.
33. I bring the blood of Jesus on every evidence that can be tendered by wicked spirits against me.
34. I file a counter-report in the heavens against every evil marriage, in the name of Jesus. to you spirit wife/ husband that there is no vacancy for you in my life, in the name of Jesus.
35. O Lord, make me a vehicle of deliverance.

36. I come by faith to mount Zion Lord, command deliverance upon my life now.
37. Lord, water me from the waters of God.
38. Let the careful siege of the enemy be dismantled, in Jesus name.
39. O Lord, defend your interest in my life.
40. Everything, written against me in the cycle of the moon, be blotted out, in Jesus name.
41. Everything, programmed into the sun, moon and stars against me, be dismantled, in
42. Jesus name.
43. Every evil thing programmed into my genes, be blotted out by the blood of Jesus.
44. O Lord, shake out seasons of failure and frustrations from my life.
45. I overthrow every wicked law, working against my life, in the name of Jesus.
46. I ordain a new time, season and profitable law, in Jesus name.
47. I speak destruction unto the palaces of the queen of the coast and of the rivers, in Jesus name.
48. I speak destruction unto the headquarters of the spirit of Egypt and blow up their altars, in the name of Jesus.
49. I speak destruction unto the altars, speaking against the purpose of God for my life, in Jesus name.
50. I declare myself a virgin for the Lord, in Jesus name.
51. Let every evil veil upon my life be torn open, in Jesus name.

52. Every wall between me and the visitation of God, be broken, in the name of Jesus.
53. Let the counsel of God prosper in my life, in the name of Jesus.
54. I destroy the power of any demonic seed in my life from the womb, in the name of Jesus.
55. I speak unto my umbilical gate to overthrow all negative parental spirits, in the name of Jesus.
56. I break the yoke of the spirit, having access to my reproductive gates, in the name of Jesus.
57. O Lord, let your time of refreshing come upon me.
58. I bring fire from the altar of the Lord upon every evil marriage, in the name of Jesus.
59. I redeem myself by the blood of Jesus from every sex trap, in the name of Jesus.
60. I erase the engraving of my name on any evil marriage record, in the name of Jesus.
61. I reject and renounce every evil spiritual marriage, in the name of Jesus.
62. I confess that Jesus is my original spouse and is jealous over me.
63. I issue a bill of divorcement to every spirit wife/ husband, in the name of Jesus.
64. I bind ever spirit wife/ husband with everlasting chains, in the name of Jesus.
65. Let heavenly testimony overcome every evil testimony of hell, in the name of Jesus.

66. O Lord, bring to my remembrance every spiritual trap and contract. certificates and destroy your rings, in Jesus name.
67. I execute judgment against water spirits and declare that you are reserved for everlasting chains in darkness, in Jesus name.
68. O Lord, contend with those who are contending with me.
69. Every trademark of water spirit, be shaken out of my life, in the name of Jesus.

Everyday! DECLARATION ON THAT SAND:

(HOLD the sand firmly and take the following prayers). Declare it as many times as your spirit tells you to stop. O LORD, anoint this sand in the name of the Father, the Son and of the Holy Spirit. Let the dew of heaven trouble this sand now. I cover the sand with the blood of Jesus. O You sand, hear the word of the Lord, I separate myself from the territorial powers using the sand to programme the steps of my destiny. Just as Moses stretch out thy rod, and smite the dust of the land, that it may become lice throughout all the land of Egypt (Exodus 8:16:17), O ye sand, I send you an errand into the kingdom of darkness, become a weapon of attacks on my enemies after the order of Moses against the Egyptians and Pharaoh (Ex 9:8-9, in Jesus name. Every power using the sand to control my life and destiny, die, in the name of Jesus, Every power blowing the sand against my life, location (mention it), backfire, in the name of Jesus.

I separate myself from the limitation of my environment. I break myself from every bondage that afflict men in my house, office, business etc You this sand, as I sprinkle it back to the earth (ground), it shall break forth the bands of wickedness upon my life (Ex 9:8-10), in Jesus name. As I sprinkle it back to the dust, every of my problem is over. As I sprinkle this sand in my environment, let all demonic presence disappear! As I sprinkle this sand back to the earth, it shall bring restoration to me, in Jesus name.

NOTES

1. Olukoya, Dr. D.K. (1999). Quotes from *Prayer Rain*. Lagos: Mountain of Fire and Miracles Ministries.

AUTHOR INFORMATION

 Pastor J.E. Charles is the Founder and Senior Pastor of the Upper Room Fire Prayer Ministries and the Dunamis Christian Community Center, a non-denominational, Spirit-led, multi-cultural Christian organization in California, preaching the gospel of Jesus Christ.

His focus remains on passionate prayer to assist with deliverance and healing of people who are physically, emotionally, and spiritually sick. Some call him "a warrior to the core" when it comes to battling demonic and ungodly powers. His dedication to evangelizing, teaching, and preaching focus on a type of violent spiritual warfare. His motto states "The violent taketh it by force."

Pastor J. E. Charles came from a culture of overt battles with generational demonic forces that had established firm grasps of control over multiple connected people. He believes that open confrontation works best to take on the forces of darkness. He sees his mission as a way to teach and guide Christians to make bold, violent struggles against demonic threats. In turn, he will guide them to discover godly breakthroughs within themselves, their families, and communities.

`His leadership positions include Intercessory Prayer and Freedom Ministries at the Well Christian Community Church, a Minister with the Redeemed Christian Church of God (RCCG), and Mountain of Fire and Miracles Ministries in California. People who know him well bestowed upon the nickname, "Mr. Prayer."

Through these leadership roles, he offers insight into deliverance, wisdom as a prophet, godly ministry, and assists you to understand the revelations that affect your personal life. His goal is to align your life and spirit with God's word and power.

The glory of God's vision exists in Pastor J. E. Charles' heart, which allows him to serve the Dunamis Christian Community most fully. The deliverance and healing teams reach out and affect those who are trapped by ungodly forces and held captive by their sin. His ministry and that of the other leaders leads others to accept Christ, welcome Him into the hearts, and live in obedience to His direction.

Pastor J. E. Charles also delivers public speaking engagements, coaches people spiritually, has authored books and offers business management consultancy services.

Isaiah 5:13: "Therefore my people are gone into captivity, because they have no knowledge: and their honorable men are famished, and their multitude dried up with thirst."

Psalm 7:9: "Oh, let the wickedness of the wicked come to an end, but establish just."

Obadiah 1:17 "But upon Mount Zion shall be [deliverance], and there shall be holiness, and the house of Jacob shall possess their possession."

MORE BOOKS FROM J.E CHARLES

  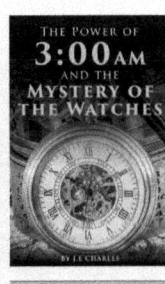 

www.ingramcontent.com/pod-product-compliance
Lightning Source LLC
Chambersburg PA
CBHW050528170426
43201CB00013B/2122